Understanding the Science of Climate Change
Talking Points – Impacts to the Great Lakes

Natural Resource Report NPS/NRPC/CCRP/NRR—2010/247

Amanda Schramm
National Park Service Pacific West Region
909 First Avenue
Seattle, WA 98104

Rachel Loehman
Rocky Mountain Research Station
Fire Sciences Laboratory
5775 West US Hwy 10
Missoula, MT 59808-9361

With special thanks to the US Forest Service's Rocky Mountain Research Station and contributions from (in alphabetical order): Jay Austin, Gregg Bruff, Hannah Campbell, Maria Caffrey, Louise Hose, Bob Krumenaker, Brent Lofgren, Mark Lynott, Joy Marburger, Jerrilyn Thompson and Leigh Welling. Layout and design: Sara Melena, Angie Richman, Caitlin Shenk, and Katherine Stehli.

September 2010

U.S. Department of the Interior
National Park Service
Natural Resource Program Center
Fort Collins, Colorado

The Natural Resource Publication series addresses natural resource topics of interest and applicability to a broad readership in the National Park Service and to others in the management of natural resources, including the scientific community, the public, and the NPS conservation and environmental constituencies. Manuscripts are peer-reviewed to ensure the information is scientifically credible, technically accurate, appropriately written for the intended audience, and is designed and published in a professional manner.

Natural Resource Reports are the designated medium for disseminating high priority, current natural resource management information with managerial application. The series targets a general, diverse audience, and may contain NPS policy considerations or address sensitive issues of management applicability. Examples of the diverse array of reports published in this series include vital signs monitoring plans; monitoring protocols; "how to" resource management papers; proceedings of resource management workshops or conferences; annual reports of resource programs or divisions of the Natural Resource Program Center; resource action plans; fact sheets; and regularly-published newsletters.

Views, statements, findings, conclusions, recommendations and data in this report are solely those of the author(s) and do not necessarily reflect views and policies of the U.S. Department of the Interior, National Park Service. Mention of trade names or commercial products does not constitute endorsement or recommendation for use by the U.S. Government.

This report is available from the Natural Resource Publications Management website:
(http://www.nature.nps.gov/publications/NRPM)

Please cite this publication as:

Schramm, A and R. Loehman. 2010. Understanding the science of climate change: talking points - impacts to the Great Lakes. Natural Resource Report NPS/NRPC/CCRP/NRR—2010/247. National Park Service, Fort Collins, Colorado.

NRInfo Reference URL: http://nrinfo/Reference.mvc/Profile?code=2165147

Climate Change Response Program webpage: http://www.nps.gov/climatechange/docs/GreatLakesTP.pdf

NPS 920/105620, September 2010

Contents

I. Introduction

Purpose

Climate change presents significant risks to our nation's natural and cultural resources. Although climate change was once believed to be a future problem, there is now unequivocal scientific evidence that our planet's climate system is warming (IPCC 2007a). While many people understand that human emissions of greenhouse gases have significantly contributed to recent observed climate changes, fewer are aware of the specific impacts these changes will bring. This document is part of a series of bio-regional summaries that provide key scientific findings about climate change and impacts to protected areas. The information is intended to provide a basic understanding of the science of climate change, known and expected impacts to resources and visitor experience, and actions that can be taken to mitigate and adapt to change. The statements may be used to communicate with managers, frame interpretive programs, and answer general questions from the public and the media. They also provide helpful information to consider in developing sustainability strategies and long-term management plans.

Audience

The Talking Points documents are primarily intended to provide park and refuge area managers and staff with accessible, up-to-date information about climate change and climate change impacts to the resources they protect.

Organizational Structure

Following the Introduction are three major sections of the document: a Regional Section that provides information on changes to the Great Lakes, a section outlining No Regrets Actions that can be taken now to mitigate and adapt to climate changes, and a general section on Global Climate Change. The Regional Section is organized around seven types of changes or impacts, while the Global Section is arranged around four topics.

Regional Section

- Temperature
- The Water Cycle (including precipitation, snow, ice, and lake levels)
- Vegetation (plant cover, species range shifts, and phenology)
- Wildlife (aquatic and terrestrial animals, range shifts, invasive species, migration, and phenology)
- Disturbance (including range shifts, plant cover, plant pests and pathogens, fire, flooding, and erosion)
- Cultural Resources
- Visitor Experience

Global Section

- Temperature and Greenhouse Gases
- Water, Snow, and Ice
- Vegetation and Wildlife
- Disturbance

Information contained in this document is derived from the published results of a range of scientific research including historical data, empirical (observed) evidence, and model projections (which may use observed or theoretical relationships). While all of the statements are informed by science, not all statements carry the same level of confidence or scientific certainty. Identifying uncertainty is an important part of science but can be a major source of confusion for decision makers and the public. In the strictest sense, all scientific results carry some level of uncertainty because the scientific method can only "prove" a hypothesis to be false. However, in a practical world, society routinely elects to make choices and select options for actions that carry an array of uncertain outcomes.

The statements in this document have been organized to help managers and their staffs differentiate among current levels of uncertainty in climate change science. In doing so, the document aims to be consistent with the language and approach taken in the Fourth Assessment on Climate Change reports by the Intergovernmental Panel on Climate Change. However, this document discriminates among only three different levels of uncertainty and does not attempt to ascribe a specific probability to any particular level. These are qualitative rather than quantitative categories, ranked from greatest to least certainty, and are based on the following:

- "What scientists know" are statements based on measurable data and historical records. These are statements for which scientists generally have high confidence and agreement because they are based on actual measurements and observations. Events under this category have already happened or are very likely to happen in the future.

- "What scientists think is likely" represents statements beyond simple facts; these are derived from some level of reasoning or critical thinking. They result from projected trends, well tested climate or ecosystem models, or empirically observed relationships (statistical comparisons using existing data).

- "What scientists think is possible" are statements that use a higher degree of inference or deduction than the previous categories. These are based on research about processes that are less well understood, often involving dynamic interactions among climate and complex ecosystems. However, in some cases, these statements represent potential future conditions of greatest concern, because they may carry the greatest risk to protected area resources.

II.   Climate Change Impacts to the Great Lakes

The Great Lakes bioregion that is discussed in this section is shown in the map to the right. A list of parks and refuges for which this analysis is most useful is included on the next page. To help the reader navigate this section, each category is designated by color-coded tabs on the outside edge of the document.

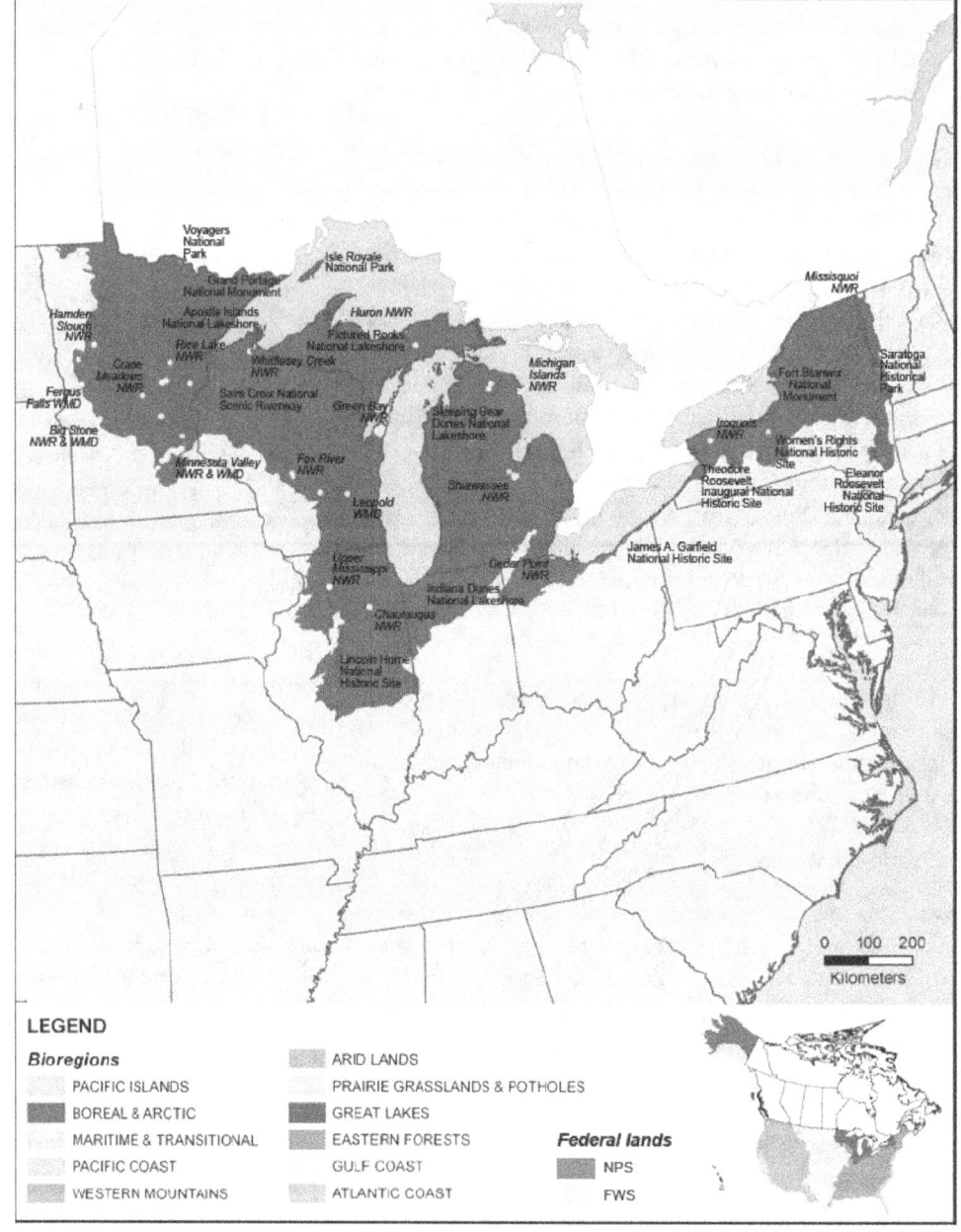

LEGEND

Bioregions

PACIFIC ISLANDS

BOREAL & ARCTIC

MARITIME & TRANSITIONAL

PACIFIC COAST

WESTERN MOUNTAINS

ARID LANDS

PRAIRIE GRASSLANDS & POTHOLES

GREAT LAKES

EASTERN FORESTS

GULF COAST

ATLANTIC COAST

Federal lands

NPS

FWS

Summary

The Great Lakes region is experiencing climatic changes including increased air and water temperatures, changes in precipitation patterns, and a reduction in winter ice. These changes have resultant effects on the natural ecosystems and cultural resources within and surrounding the lakes, as well as area recreational opportunities. Warmer lake waters are leading to extended periods of lake stratification, which in turn can reduce the water's suitability for native coldwater fish species and the species they rely on for food. As surface water temperatures warm, some fish species are expected to migrate northward toward colder waters, or else suffer population declines. Invasive species from outside the Great Lakes may increasingly find suitable conditions within the Lakes as conditions change, further threatening the livelihood of native species. Lake-effect snow may see a reduction as both air and water temperatures warm. Less snow in general is likely to impact the winter recreational season, which may also be reduced overall as the cold season shortens. Warmer temperatures and reduced ice are expected to increase evaporation, leading to lower lake levels and associated impacts on recreational boating. Changes in the precipitation and flooding cycle may lead to significant increases in water contamination from flooded sewage systems. Lower lake levels as well as changes in moisture, wind, soil chemistry and storm frequency may expose archeological resources or negatively affect their preservation.

Temperature

Water Cycle

Vegetation

Wildlife

Disturbance

Cultural Resources

Visitor Experience

List of Parks and Refuges

Temperature

Water Cycle

Vegetation

Wildlife

Disturbance

Cultural Resources

Visitor Experience

U.S. National Park Service Units
- Apostle Islands NL
- Delaware Water Gap NRA
- Eleanor Roosevelt NHS
- Fort Stanwix NM
- Grand Portage NM
- Home of Frankiln D Roosevelt NHS
- Hopewell Furnace NHS
- Indiana Dunes NL
- Isle Royale NP
- James A. Garfield NHS
- Keweenaw NHP
- Lincoln Home NHS
- Martin Van Buren NHS
- Mississippi National River & Recreation Area
- Perry's Victory and International Peace Memorial NME
- Pictured Rocks NL
- Saint Croix NSR
- Saratoga NHP
- Sleeping Bear Dunes NL
- Steamtown NHS
- Theodore Roosevelt Inaugural NHS
- Thomas Cole NHS
- Vanderbilt Mansion NHS
- Voyageurs NP
- Women's Rights NHP

U.S. Fish & Wildlife Service Units
- Agassiz NWR
- Big Stone NWR & WMD
- Cedar Point NWR
- Chautauqua NWR
- Crane Meadows NWR
- Detroit Lakes WMD
- Detroit River NWR
- Emiquon NWR
- Erie NWR
- Fergus Falls WMD
- Fox River NWR
- Glacial Ridge NWR
- Gravel Island NWR
- Green Bay NWR
- Hamden Slough NWR
- Harbor Island NWR
- Horicon NWR
- Huron NWR
- Iroquois NWR
- Leopold WMD
- Litchfield WMD
- Michigan WMD
- Michigan Islands NWR
- Mille Lacs NWR
- Minnesota Valley NWR & WMD
- Missisquoi NWR
- Montezuma NWR
- Morris WMD
- Necedah NWR
- Northern Tallgrass Prairie NWR
- Ottawa NWR
- Rice Lake NWR
- Rydell NWR
- Seney NWR
- Sherburne NWR
- Shiawassee NWR
- St. Croix WMD
- Tamarac NWR
- Trempealeau NWR
- Upper Mississipi NWFR
- West Sister Island NWR
- Whittlesey Creek NWR

Acronym	Unit Type
NHP	National Historic Park
NHS	National Historic Site
NL	National Lakeshore
NM	National Monument
NME	National Memorial
NP	National Park
NRA	National Recreation Area
NSR	National Scenic Riverway
NWFR	National Wildlife and Fish Refuge
NWR	National Wildlife Refuge
WMD	Wetland Management District

A. Temperature

What scientists know....

- The northern Midwest, including the upper Great Lakes region, warmed by almost 4°F (2°C) in the 20th century (NAST 2000).

- Based on historical records, extreme heat events are occurring more frequently in the Great Lakes region (NAST 2000, Wuebbles et al. 2003).

- Data for Lakes Michigan, Huron and Superior show that summer water temperatures are rising. Lake Superior's summer surface water temperatures increased by 4.5°F (2.5°C) between 1979 and 2006, a rate approximately double the rate of air temperature rise during the same period. An earlier start of the stratified season significantly increases the period over which the lake warms during the summer months, leading to a stronger mean summer temperature trend than would be expected from changes in summer air temperature alone (Austin and Colman 2007).

- Over 15 years leading up to 2002, two-thirds of the winters in the Midwest had temperatures above the long-term historical winter average. The last spring frost is coming earlier and the first autumn frost is coming later (Kling et al. 2003, Wuebbles and Hayhoe 2003).

- Between 1968 and 2002, mean annual air temperature increased at an average rate of 0.037 °C (0.067°F) per year at lakes Huron, Erie and Ontario, resulting in an overall 1.3 °C (2.3°F) increase for the 34-year period. August surface water temperature has risen 0.084 °C annually at Lake Huron and 0.048 °C (0.086°F) annually at Lake Ontario, resulting in overall increases of 2.9 °C (5.22°F) and 1.6 °C (2.88°F), respectively, for the same time period. Temperatures at Lake Erie rose a small, but not significant, amount over the 34-year span (Dobiesz and Lester 2009).

What scientists think is likely...

- Climatic model predictions consistently indicate warming in the region (Kling et al. 2003, Wuebbles et al. 2003).

What scientists think is possible...

- Warming is expected to vary across the Midwest. Different models and scenarios show different patterns of warming, with one model showing an increased warming at higher latitudes, and another showing more warming at lower latitudes (Wuebbles et al. 2003).

- Based on climate model predictions, summer temperatures in the Great Lakes region are projected to rise by at least 5°F (3°C), and as much as 20° F (11°C) by 2100. Depending on the model and the scenario (high, mid-range or low carbon emission predictions), the projected temperature changes vary (Kling et al. 2003, Wuebbles et al. 2003).

- Summer temperature changes are likely to show the greatest increase in the southern and western part of the Midwest (Wuebbles et al. 2003).

- Models project that by 2071–2100, modeling suggests that annual water temperature may increase in all of the Great Lakes, with the most change in Lake Superior and the least in Lake Erie. Summer surface water temperatures are expected to increase by up to 6°C (10.8°F) on average (Trumpickas et al. 2009).

This graphic demonstrates the shift in average minimum temperatures in the great lakes from 1990-2006. Photo courtesy of the National Arbor Day Foundation.

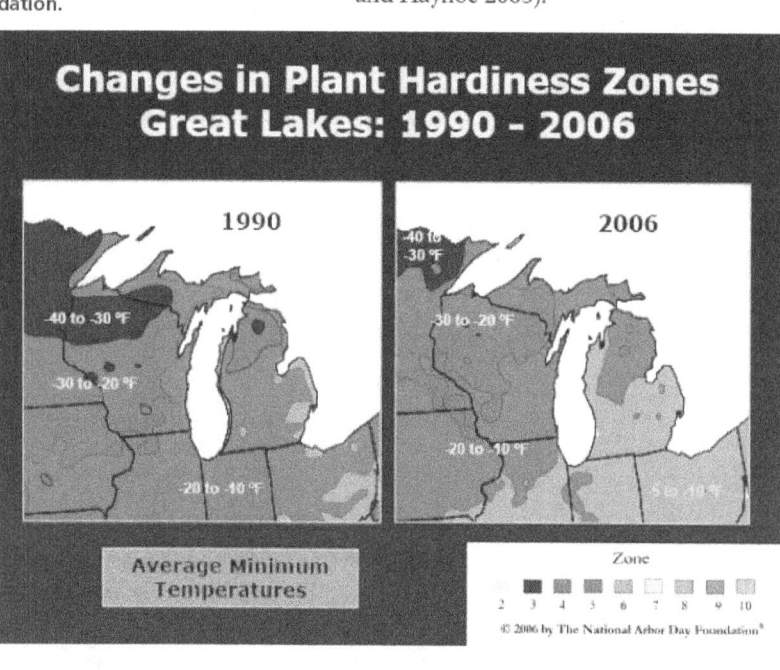

Temperature

Water Cycle

Vegetation

Wildlife

Disturbance

Cultural Resources

Visitor Experience

Lake level fluctuations in the great lakes prior to 1980 were predominantly driven by changes in precipitation; however, evaporation has begun to significantly contribute to lake level changes for the first time on record. Decrease in lake levels on Lake Superior in Apostle Islands National Lakeshore; NPS photo.

- The average date when spring temperatures warm to 10°C (50°F) in the Great Lakes region is projected to advance 24 to 47 days, while the date when fall temperatures drop to 10°C (50°F) is also projected to advance 18 to 51 days by 2071-2100 (Trumpickas et al. 2009).

B. THE WATER CYCLE

What scientists know....

- Ice around the Great Lakes and tributary streams is declining and melting earlier (Robertson et al. 1992, Anderson et al. 1996, Magnuson et al. 2000, Austin and Colman 2007).

- The timing of Lake Superior's summer overturn advanced two weeks between 1979 and 2006. On average the date of the summer overturn has been half a day earlier each year (Austin and Colman 2007).

- Based on historical records, winter precipitation is becoming more variable than summer precipitation (Wuebbles et al. 2003).

- Lake level fluctuations in Lakes Michigan and Huron prior to 1980 were predominantly driven by changes in precipitation; however, evaporation has begun to signifi-

cantly contribute to lake level changes for the first time on record. Increasing summer water surface temperatures, which correlate with decreasing winter ice cover, have caused evaporation rates to more than double since 1980 (Hanrahan et al. 2010).

- Based on historical data, Lakes Huron, Erie, Michigan, and Ontario experienced a statistically significant trend toward increased precipitation between the years 1930 and 2000. During the same time period, streamflows increased in three connecting channels of the Great Lakes: the St. Clair, Niagara and St. Lawrence rivers (McBean and Motiee 2008).

- In Bayfield Wisconsin between 1857 and 2007, the onset of ice cover occurred an average of 1.6 days later per decade, and break-up of ice cover has occurred an average of 1.7 days earlier per decade due to rising air and water temperatures. Taken together, these changes have resulted in an approximately 3-day per decade (45 days over 150 years) reduction in the ice cover period. The most significant changes influencing this average occurred since 1975, with the ice season beginning an average of 11.7 days later and ending 3.0 days earlier every decade (Howk 2009).

Temperature

Water Cycle

Vegetation

Wildlife

Disturbance

Cultural Resources

Visitor Experience

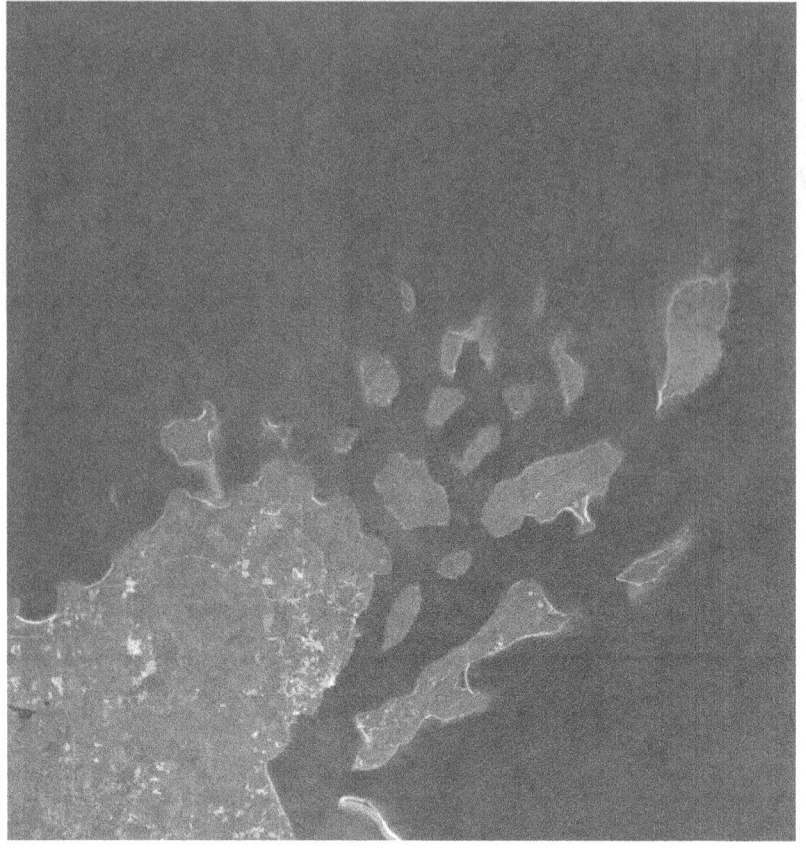

This is an image of Lake Superior in Apostle Islands National Lakeshore, whose record low water occurred in 2007 when the lake was 22 inches below full. Photo courtesy of NASA LandSat and prepared by Neil Howk.

- In Minnesota, measurements of streamflow based on 53 to 101 years of historical records in the years leading up to 2002 show increase in peak flows due to summer rainfall events. The number of high flow days also increased. Summer and winter base flow increased significantly, likely due to wetter summers and more frequent snow melt events due to warmer winters. Mean annual flow rates changed at a rate of 2% per year over the last 50 years of record, increasing to 8% per year over the last 15 years (Novotny and Stefan 2007).

What scientists think is likely...

- Declines in lake winter ice are expected to continue (Wuebbles et al. 2003).

- Warmer temperatures and reduced lake ice cover and duration of cover could cause an increase in evaporation (Lofgren et al. 2002, Wuebbles et al. 2003).

- Lake-effect snowfall, which relies on frigid winter air temperatures and warmer water temperatures, is an important factor for the vitality of mesic vegetation. Reductions in snowfall due to higher air tem-

peratures predicted as a result of climate change may result in a major decrease in the abundance of ecologically and economically important species such as Sugar maple (*Acer Saccharum*) (Henne et al. 2007).

- The duration of winter ice may become shorter in the Great Lakes. Warming temperatures could cause earlier ice melt and change stream peak flow, potentially increasing flood risk from spring rainfall (Kling et al. 2003, Austin and Colman 2007).

- Based on historical records, a 2007 study found that at the current rate of winter ice decline, Lake Superior could have periods of little to no open-lake ice during a typical winter within three decades (Austin and Colman 2007).

- A reduction in ice cover coupled with warmer temperatures is likely to lead to higher levels of evaporation, which could result in up to a 2-foot lowering of lake levels (USGCRP 2009).

- The Great Lakes region will likely grow drier overall. Any increases in precipitation will likely be counterbalanced by increased evaporation due to temperature increases (Kling et al. 2003). Intense short-duration rain storms are projected to occasionally break periods of drought (UCS 2003).

What scientists think is possible...

- Winter precipitation is expected to increase in the Midwest. Summer precipitation is expected to stay the same or decrease (Wuebbles et al. 2003).

- Groundwater levels may decrease. Models show some decreases in aquifers and an expansion of dewatered areas (Lofgren et al. 2002).

- The maximum duration of lake stratification in the Great Lakes could increase by as much as 90 days as summer temperatures warm. Such an effect could reduce suitability for coldwater fish species (Lehman 2002, Kling et al. 2003, Trumpickas et al. 2009).

Temperature

Water Cycle

Vegetation

Wildlife

Disturbance

Cultural Resources

Visitor Experience

Temperature

Water Cycle

Vegetation

Wildlife

Disturbance

Cultural Resources

Visitor Experience

Dominant Forest Types

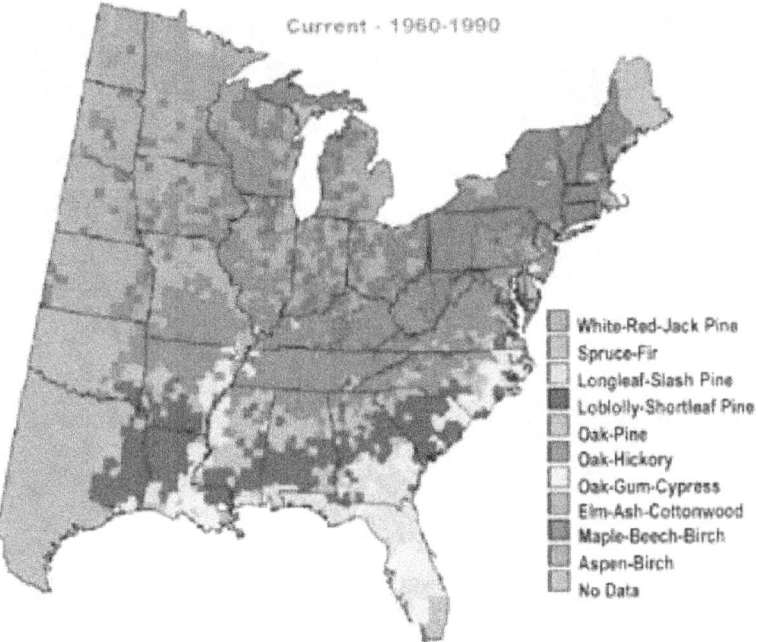

Current · 1960-1990

White-Red-Jack Pine
Spruce-Fir
Longleaf-Slash Pine
Loblolly-Shortleaf Pine
Oak-Pine
Oak-Hickory
Oak-Gum-Cypress
Elm-Ash-Cottonwood
Maple-Beech-Birch
Aspen-Birch
No Data

Dominant Forest Types

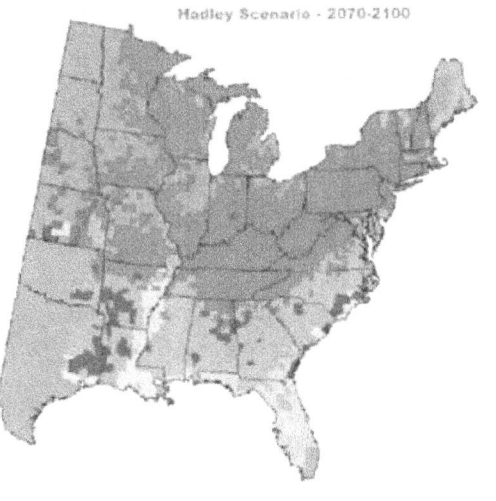

Hadley Scenario · 2070-2100

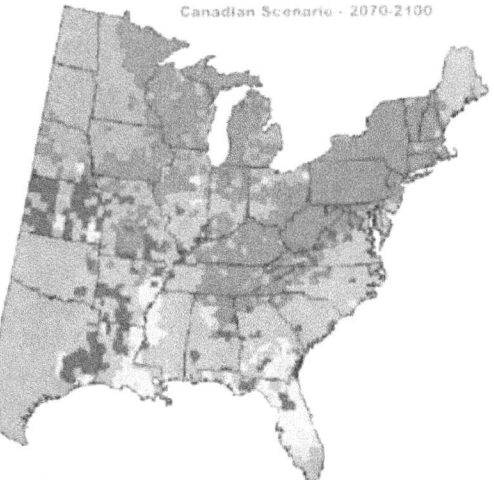

Canadian Scenario · 2070-2100

These images show current forest types (top) compared to projected forest shift (bottom) due to climate change. Images courtesy of USFS.

C. VEGETATION

What scientists know....

- The growing season has been expanding as spring arrives sooner. The average length of winter freeze has been decreasing, with frost days declining in the U.S. The first freeze occurring later and last freeze occurring earlier has expanded the growing season (Wuebbles et al. 2003).

- Increasing levels of carbon dioxide affect the physiology of vegetation (Watson et al. 1997).

- Cool adapted tree species, such as sugar maple and birch, are projected to have smaller habitat in the northeastern U.S., shifting largely to Canada. Oaks, hickories, and pines may see an expansion of potential habitats, although expansion may be limited by soil and seed dispersal (Watson et al. 1997, USDA 2001, Parmesan 2006).

What scientists think is likely...

- Increasing carbon dioxide levels could increase the productivity of trees and the efficiency with which they use nitrogen (Watson et al. 1997).

- Warming temperatures can increase problems related to insects and disease. Because insects and pathogens have shorter life spans than most forest vegetation, they can respond more rapidly to climate change. A longer growing season may mean that more generations of pests can attack vegetation, while a shorter and warmer winter will mean more successful over-wintering for pests. If vegetation has been stressed by drought or fire, it is also more susceptible to disease and infestation (Watson et al. 1996, Winnett 1998, USDA 2001, Hayhoe et al. 2007).

- Wild rice is likely to be adversely affected. Deep or flooding waters in the early spring could delay germination of seed, leading to crop failures. Lower water levels late in summer could cause wild rice stalks to break under the weight of the fruithead or could make rice beds inaccessible to harvesters. Extended droughts could lead to more competition with other shallow water species (NAST 2000).

- Increased variability of temperature and precipitation could be harmful to vegetation and could cause diebacks. Climate change models predict higher temperature maxima and more extreme precipitation events. As plants rely on specific ranges of temperature and precipitation, longer droughts, more flooding events and heat waves outside of their normal range would stress them. In addition, winters with warm snaps may cause trees and other vegetation to come out of dormancy, which would increase their vulnerability to further cold temperatures (Winnett 1998, USDA 2001).

- Future species migrations may differ from the past due to habitat loss and fragmentation, reducing the natural system's ability to respond to global change. In the past, species have migrated through intact forests. With human development, there are fewer forested sites and individuals within a population. This will likely make migration of species adapting to temperature and precipitation changes more difficult (Iverson et al. 2004).

- Increased water temperatures enhance biological productivity, which decreases dissolved oxygen, and could increase the growth of undesirable species, such as algae blooms (Poff et al. 2002).

What scientists think is possible...

- Shorter winters and warming temperatures may lead to invasive species, pests, and pathogens and cause redistribution of tree species and significant alteration of ecosystems (Iverson and Prasad 2002, Wuebbles et al. 2003).

- Forest species composition is projected to change. Bayfield Peninsula (Wisconsin, near Apostle Islands NL) forest composition is modeled to respond to a 5°C (9°F) increase in annual temperature by changing from a northern hardwood/boreal mix to more southern species (He et al. 2002). Paper birch habitat is modeled to virtually disappear from the area under some greenhouse gas scenarios (Prasad 1999).

- Predicting the rate of forest composition change has proven difficult, although some species may not easily adapt if climate change occurs as rapidly as predicted (Thompson et al. 1998, Wuebbles et al. 2003).

- Warmer temperatures may exacerbate the effects of ozone on forest growth, including reduced growth, reduced seed production and increased vulnerability to disease (Watson et al. 1997, USDA 2001).

- Boreal forests in the Boundary Waters Canoe Area Wilderness of Minnesota, many of which exist at the edge of their ranges, are expected to give way to grassland/savanna or temperate hardwood forest in the next century (Frelich and Reich 2009).

(Top) Spraying for invasive spotted knapweed at Pictured Rocks NL, NPS photo.

(Bottom) Decreased water levels have already begun to affect vegetation in the great lakes. Image courtesy of Northern Wisconsin Daily Press.

Bad River wild rice harvest cancelled

By Chad Dally
Thursday, August 09th, 2007 10:35:05 AM

Leah Gibala/Submitted Photo
Bad River tribal members Donald Corbine and his son, Justin, harvest wild rice in the Kakagon Slough in August, 2006.

The fears of many Bad River tribal members have been realized: For the first time in history, there will be no harvest of wild rice this year within tribal boundaries.

The Bad River Tribal Council announced on Wednesday that, due to extremely low water levels, a one-year hiatus is in place for rice beds in the 12,000-acre Kakagon, Bad River and Bad River Slough complexes, as well on Honest John Lake and the Sand Cut Sloughs off of Oak Point.

"This is something we have to do as a people," said Matt O'Claire, a game warden with Bad River's Natural Resources Department (NRD). "...It's something that we share with everybody, but we also talk about looking ahead seven generations and the need to protect it for our children and grandchildren."

Temperature

Water Cycle

Vegetation

Wildlife

Disturbance

Cultural Resources

Visitor Experience

Temperature

Water Cycle

Vegetation

Wildlife

Disturbance

Cultural Resources

Visitor Experience

D. WILDLIFE

What scientists know....

(Top) American Badger was first recorded at Pictured Rocks NL in 2004. Photo of tranquilized badger undergoing radio collaring; NPS photo.

(Bottom) Henry Quinlan, Fish and Wildlife Service Fisheries biologist weighs a lake sturgeon along the Bad River in Wisconsin. This fish species is an important biological component of the Great Lakes fish community and is listed as either threatened or endangered. The lake sturgeon may have a hard time coping with climate change. FWS photo.

- Under either forest expansion or contraction, relative mixtures of species in forest communities will change. This may cause some animal species to be at risk. Greater rates of change are associated with greater disequilibrium between the habitat needs of the species and the habitat realities (i.e., temperature and precipitation) (Watson et al. 1997, Parmesan and Yohe 2003).

- Changes in climate are having significant effects on breeding and winter distribution of birds in North America (Watson et al. 1997).

What scientists think is likely...

- Distribution of fish may change according to the temperature of water. Warm water fish populations are projected to expand northward, while cold water fish populations could decrease (Wuebbles et al. 2003, Sharma et al. 2007).

- Warmer temperatures may increase the length of summer stratification in lakes in the Great Lakes region, creating deep water, oxygen-depleted areas. This change would negatively impact cold water fish in the lakes (Lehman 2002, Kling et al. 2003).

- As spring arrives earlier, mosquitoes and black flies could begin hatching earlier in the season and may take longer to die off as winters become shorter (Reither 2001).

- Earlier springs and later winters may disrupt the timing between lifecycles of predators and prey (Parmesan 2006).

- In Michigan, one study has shown that some species of migratory birds are arriving significantly earlier than in the past. Although these species appear capable of adapting, they rely heavily on specific vegetation. If the vegetation cannot respond to climatic changes, the appropriate vegetation may not be available when the birds arrive (USGCRP 1996).

- Increasing temperatures and potential storminess could disrupt the shallow waters where many fish spawn. These changes would threaten population levels of native fish (Poff et al. 2002).

- In 2002, western Lake Erie became temporarily stratified due to an unusually warm summer. The affected area was a region with maximum depth of 10m in which stratification is very rare, but did occur during a period (about a week) of very low wind. The resulting low dissolved oxygen levels near the lake floor were linked to a failure of fall recruitment for Burrowing mayflies (Hexagenia spp.), an important food resource for yellow perch and a major indicator species of the ecological condition of the lake. A trend toward more frequent hot summers in the Great Lakes

Several Great Lakes may be vulnerable to aquatic invasive species from the Caspian Sea like the Zebra Mussel found in Sleeping Bear Dunes National Lakeshore; NPS photo.

- As lake temperatures increase and the ecosystem is stressed by changing climatic conditions, the number of exotic species, such as zebra mussels and sea lamprey, are projected to increase. Zebra mussels add to increased productivity in lakes by outcompeting native species and increasing water clarity that leads to accelerated algae growth (Poff et al. 2002).

- Warming temperatures and vegetation changes may result in increased deer populations at Minnesota's Boundary Waters Canoe Area Wilderness (Frelich and Reich 2009).

E. DISTURBANCE

What scientists know....

- Changing runoff patterns result in changing stream channel erosion and deposition patterns (Pruski and Nearing 2002).

- Increasing summer air and surface water temperatures coupled with a reduction in the temperature gradient between air and water are destabilizing the atmospheric surface layer above Lake Superior, resulting in a 5% per decade increase in surface wind speeds above the lake (Desai et al. 2009).

- In Minnesota, recent mild winters have led to a rapid population growth of eastern larch beetle (Dendroctonus simplex LeConte), which has resulted in significant mortality for Minnesota Larch stands (Frelich and Reich 2009).

- A model based on historical voltinism (number of generations bred per year) for grape berry moth (Paralobesia viteana Clemens) under varying scenarios of climate change in Lake Erie and other large lakes shows that increases in mean surface temperatures >2°C can significantly affect insect voltinism (Tobin et al. 2008).

- A coastal vulnerability assessment of 22 coastal national parks found that Great Lakes shorelines are considered moderately vulnerable (Pendleton et al. 2010).

region could lead to recurrent loss of mayfly larvae in shallow areas in this and other Great Lakes (Bridgeman et al. 2006).

What scientists think is possible...

- National parks may not be able to meet their mandate of protecting current biodiversity within park boundaries for mammals. Park wildlife, able to move northward or to higher elevation to avoid global warming impacts, may be forced out of the parks and into unprotected habitats (Burns et al. 2003).

- Due to vegetation shifts, and thus habitat shifts, parks may experience a shift in mammalian species greater than anything documented in the geologic record. This prediction is based on the idea that species will change location as a group. Several researchers have concluded that rapid changes on the order of 20 to 50 years are possible (Burns et al. 2003).

- Specific changes in mammal populations and movements may be hard to predict due to the complexity of their interactions with the environment and the rapid pace of change that is expected (Burns et al. 2003).

Temperature

Water Cycle

Vegetation

Wildlife

Disturbance

Cultural Resources

Visitor Experience

Temperature

Water Cycle

Vegetation

Wildlife

Disturbance

Cultural Resources

Visitor Experience

What scientists think is likely...

- Changing precipitation patterns and accompanying lowering of groundwater tables may result in alterations to the drainage pattern, including renewed or accelerated stream bed incision and channel wall erosion, increased sediment transportation and deposition, and drying out of wetlands (Tucker and Slingerland 1997, Winter 2000).

- Modeling suggests that the increasing wind speeds on Lake Superior may lead to increases in water current speeds, and long-term warming can lengthen the season of stratification and cause the surface mixed layer to become shallower. Such changes may have significant implications for the biogeochemical cycles of large lakes, atmospheric circulation along lake shores, and the transport of airborne pollutants in regions with many lakes (Desai et al. 2009).

(Top) Decreasing lake levels will have an impact on park or refuge buildings and facilities, like these sunken docks at Apostle Islands National Lakeshore; NPS photo.

(Bottom) A coastal vulnerability assessment of 22 coastal national parks found that Great Lakes shorelines are considered moderately vulnerable. Erosion along sand banks on Lake Michigan in Indiana Dunes National Lakeshore; NPS photo.

- A study conducted in Lake Erie showed that external phosphorus levels could increase due to increased runoff, excretion from invasive dreissenid mussels, and other effects associated with climate change, resulting in substantial effects on freshwater ecosystem services (Roy et al. 2010).

- Near shore areas of several Great Lakes and most of Lake Erie may be vulnerable to aquatic invasive species from the Caspian Sea (Fitzpatrick and Hargrove 2009).

- Rising temperatures and earlier springs are likely to increase forest fire hazards, lengthen the fire season, and create larger fires. These changes could increase atmospheric carbon contributions from forests (Watson et al. 1997, Winnett 1998, USDA 2001, Westerling et al. 2006).

What scientists think is possible...

- Models predict an earlier spring growth and marginal increase in peak biomass of Cladophora, a form of nuisance algae, in Lake Ontario (Malkin et al. 2008).

- In southern Wisconsin, model projections of 10% to 40% increases in the strength of extreme precipitation could result in greater potential for flooding. Such flooding could be accompanied by combined sewer overflow into the Great Lakes, including a potential by 50% to 120% increase in sewer overflow into Lake Michigan by 2100 (Patz et al. 2008).

- Some resource management strategies that could lessen ecosystem disturbances (i.e., prescribed fires, assisted migrations, restoring species to wilderness) may be difficult to enact or limited in effectiveness under changed conditions, and may even be in conflict with existing policy (Frelich and Reich 2009).

Historic structures, like the Quincy Dry House at Keweenaw National Historical Park are vulnerable to changes in temperature, wind, and moisture as well as infestation of pests; NPS photo.

F. CULTURAL RESOURCES

What scientists know....

- Historic structures are vulnerable to changes in temperature, wind, and moisture as well as infestation of pests (UNESCO 2007).

- Preservation of archeological resources in the earth depends on a delicate balance of conditions. Changes to these conditions may reduce the change of artifacts' survival (UNESCO 2007).

- Benefits of using local knowledge and traditional practices in resource management can help facilitate adaptation to climate change (Finucane 2009, IPCC 2008).

- Land use areas that are fixed in place, like national parks and Native American reservations, are particularly vulnerable to the effects of climate change because they cannot adapt by relocating in response to changes in natural conditions (Smith et al. 2001).

What scientists think is possible....

- Increasing frequency and intensity of severe storms and floods may pose threats to historic structures ethnographic and archeological sites.

- Warmer water may result in accelerated biological activity and speed deterioration of submerged cultural resources or expanded anoxic conditions and help preserve the resources, such as sunken ships. The one certainty is that climate change will produce challenges to the preservation of cultural resources that have not been faced previously (Nicholls and Klein 2005).

Temperature

Water Cycle

Vegetation

Wildlife

Disturbance

Cultural Resources

Visitor Experience

Temperature

Water Cycle

Vegetation

Wildlife

Disturbance

Cultural Resources

Visitor Experience

G. VISITOR EXPERIENCE

What scientists know....

- The winter recreation season in the region is becoming shorter and less reliable overall, although some areas have experienced an increase in seasonal snowfall over the past few decades.

What scientists think is likely....

- Reduction in snowpack could significantly reduce opportunities for winter recreational activities such as skiing and snowmobiling (Scott et al. 2008).

- Shoulder seasons will likely begin and end earlier in the spring and start and continue later in the fall. Opportunities for summer activities may extend longer.

(Top) Changes in wildlife composition due to climate change will impact activities in the parks, such as fishing and bird watching; NPS photo.

(Bottom) Reduction in snowpack could significantly reduce opportunities for winter recreational activities such as skiing and snowmobiling; NPS photo.

- Changes in wildlife composition could impact activities in the parks and refuges, such as fishing and bird watching.

What scientists think is possible....

- Recreational beaches may face closure under climate change due to increased pollution and waterborne pathogens. Heavier rainfall, warmer lake waters, and lowered lake levels associated with climate change could all contribute to beach contamination (Patz et al. 2008).

- There may be increased public health risk by the likely expansion of the prevalence and range of Lyme and West Nile Virus (IPCC 2007b). Infections in foods (e.g., fish) could also increase (Patz et al. 2000).

- Longer mosquito and black fly seasons could be a nuisance to visitors and may increase the risk of mosquito-borne diseases, such as dengue, yellow fever, and West Nile virus (Patz et al. 2000, Reither 2001, IPCC 2007b).

- Lake level fluctuations may affect the viability of recreational marine boating as marina operators struggle with the expense and logistics of providing appropriate infrastructure for boaters (Wall 2008).

- Park and refuge facilities may be inadequate for new conditions. Recreational infrastructure such as fixed docks and boat ramps may be too high as lake levels decline. Shallow water at docks and anchorages may limit access by deeper-draft boats. Navigational hazards and new sand bars may be exposed. There may be pressure on managers to lengthen or lower docks or dredge shallow areas, and to mark navigational water hazards.

- Warmer waters and longer open water (non-ice) seasons may "open" boating to more people and different kinds of boats. Coupled with the increasing frequency and intensity of severe storms, however, this may lead to increasing issues of visitor safety (e.g., groundings, capsizings, etc.) and the need for more rescues by the managing agencies.

- Storms on land could create hazardous conditions and visitor injuries from falling debris, flooding, vehicle accidents, and mass wasting (i.e., landslides, mud flows, rock falls).

- Increasing frequency and intensity of severe storms and floods may pose threats to roads and trails, administrative facilities, and other park and refuge resources and infrastructure.

- Shallow lake margins could expose new land which, depending on local conditions, may become new beaches or mud flats.

- Drying of ephemeral wetlands on lake margins may adversely affect the food web that supports sport fish communities, as well as the spawning areas fish depend upon for reproduction. Migratory birds and other wetland-dependent organisms will also likely be impacted.

- Reduced groundwater and stream flows may affect the availability of high quality water to support both park and refuge ecosystems and facilities.

- Increased temperatures could hinder physical activities in parks and refuges, resulting in increased heat exhaustion.

- Increased summer temperatures could lead to increased utility expenditures in parks and refuges in the summer and, potentially, decreases in the winter.

Changes in wildlife composition due to climate change will impact activities in the parks, such as fishing and bird watching. NPS photo.

Temperature

Water Cycle

Vegetation

Wildlife

Disturbance

Cultural Resources

Visitor Experience

III. No Regrets Actions: How Individuals, Parks, Refuges, and Their Partners Can Do Their Part

Individuals, businesses, and agencies release carbon dioxide (CO_2), the principal greenhouse gas, through burning of fossil fuels for electricity, heating, transportation, food production, and other day-to-day activities. Increasing levels of atmospheric CO_2 have measurably increased global average temperatures, and are projected to cause further changes in global climate, with severe implications for vegetation, wildlife, oceans, water resources, and human populations. Emissions reduction – limiting production of CO_2 and other greenhouse gases - is an important step in addressing climate change. It is the responsibility of agencies and individuals to find ways to reduce greenhouse gas emissions and to educate about the causes and consequences of climate change, and ways in which we can reduce our impacts on natural resources. There are many simple actions that each of us can take to reduce our daily carbon emissions, some of which will even save money.

Agencies Can...

Improve sustainability and energy efficiency

- Use energy efficient products, such as ENERGY STAR® approved office equipment and light bulbs.

- Initiate an energy efficiency program to monitor energy use in buildings. Provide guidelines for reducing energy consumption. Conserve water.

- Convert to renewable energy sources such as solar or wind generated power.

- Specify "green" designs for construction of new or remodeled buildings.

- Include discussions of climate change in the park Environmental Management System.

- Conduct an emmisions inventory and set goals for CO_2 reduction.

- Provide alternative transportation options such as employee bicycles and shuttles for within-unit commuting.

- Provide hybrid electric or propane-fueled vehicles for official use, and impose fuel standards for park vehicles. Reduce the number and/or size of park vehicles and boats to maximize efficiency.

- Provide a shuttle service or another form of alternate transportation for visitor and employee travel to and within the unit.

- Provide incentives for use of alternative transportation methods.

- Use teleconferences and webinars or other forms of modern technology in place of travel to conferences and meetings.

Implement Management Actions

- Engage and enlist collaborator support (e.g., tribes, nearby agencies, private landholders) in climate change discussions, responses, adaptation and mitigation.

- Develop strategies and identify priorities for managing uncertainty surrounding climate change effects in parks and refuges.

- Dedicate funds not only to sustainable actions but also to understanding the impacts to the natural and cultural resources.

- Build a strong partnership-based foundation for future conservation efforts.

- Identify strategic priorities for climate change efforts when working with partners.

- Incorporate anticipated climate change impacts, such as decreases in lake levels or changes in vegetation and wildlife, into management plans.

An interpretive brochure about climate change impacts to National Parks was created in 2006 and was distributed widely. This brochure was updated in 2008.

Climate Change in National Parks

Park Service employees install solar panels at San Francisco Maritime National Historical Park (Top); At the National Mall, Park Service employees use clean-energy transportation to lead tours; NPS photos.

flows for fish, and maintain and develop access corridors to climate change refugia.

- Restoration efforts are important as a means for enhancing species' ability to cope with stresses and adapt to climatic and environmental changes. Through restoration of natural areas, we can lessen climate change impacts on species and their habitats. These efforts will help preserve biodiversity, natural resources, and recreational opportunities.

- Address climate change impacts to cultural resources by taking actions to document, preserve, and recover them.

Educate staff and the public

- Post climate change information in easily accessible locations such as on bulletin boards and websites.

- Provide training for park and refuge employees and partners on effects of climate change on resources, and on dissemination of climate change knowledge to the public.

- Support the development of region, park, or refuge-specific interpretive products on the impacts of climate change.

- Incorporate climate change research and information in interpretive and education outreach programming.

- Distribute up-to-date interpretive products (e.g., the National Park Service-wide Climate Change in National Parks brochure).

- Develop climate change presentations for local civic organizations, user and partner conferences, national meetings, etc.

- Incorporate climate change questions and answers into Junior Ranger programs.

- Help visitors make the connection between reducing greenhouse gas emissions and resource stewardship.

- Encourage visitors to use public or non-motorized transportation to and around parks.

- Encourage climate change research and scientific study in park units and refuges.

- Design long-term monitoring projects and management activities that do not rely solely on fossil fuel-based transportation and infrastructure.

- Incorporate products and services that address climate change in the development of all interpretive and management plans.

- Take inventory of the facilities/boundaries/species within your park or refuge that may benefit from climate change mitigation or adaptation activities.

- Participate in gateway community sustainability efforts.

- Recognize the value of ecosystem services that an area can provide, and manage the area to sustain these services. Conservation is more cost-effective than restoration and helps maintain ecosystem integrity.

- Provide recycling options for solid waste and trash generated within the park.

Restore damaged landscapes

- Strategically focus restoration efforts, both in terms of the types of restoration undertaken and their national, regional, and local scale and focus, to help maximize resilience.

- Restore and conserve connectivity within habitats, protect and enhance instream

> "Humankind has not woven the web of life. We are but one thread within it. Whatever we do to the web, we do to ourselves. All things are bound together. All things connect."
> —Chief Seattle

- Encourage visitors to reduce their carbon footprint in their daily lives and as part of their tourism experience.

Individuals can...

- In the park or refuge park their car and walk or bike. Use shuttles where available. Recycle and use refillable water bottles. Stay on marked trails to help further ecosystem restoration efforts.

- At home, walk, carpool, bike or use public transportation if possible. A full bus equates to 40 fewer cars on the road. When driving, use a fuel-efficient vehicle.

- Do not let cars or boats idle - letting a car idle for just 20 seconds burns more gasoline than turning it off and on again.

- Replace incandescent bulbs in five most frequently used light fixtures in the home with bulbs that have the ENERGY STAR® rating. If every household in the U.S. takes this one action we will prevent greenhouse gas emissions equivalent to the emissions from nearly 10 million cars, in addition to saving money on energy costs.

Reduce, Reuse, Recycle, Refuse

- Use products made from recycled paper, plastics and aluminum - these use 55-95% less energy than products made from scratch.

- Purchase a travel coffee mug and a reusable water bottle to reduce use of disposable products (Starbucks uses more than 1 billion paper cups a year).

- Carry reusable bags instead of using paper or plastic bags.

- Recycle drink containers, paper, newspapers, electronics, and other materials. Bring recyclables home for proper disposal when recycle bins are not available. Rather than taking old furniture and clothes to the dump, consider "recycling" them at a thrift store.

- Keep an energy efficient home. Purchase ENERGY STAR® appliances, properly insulate windows, doors and attics, and lower the thermostat in the winter and raise it in the summer (even 1-2 degrees makes a big difference). Switch to green power generated from renewable energy sources such as wind, solar, or geothermal.

- Buy local goods and services that minimize emissions associated with transportation.

- Encourage others to participate in the actions listed above.

- Conserve water.

For more information on how you can reduce carbon emissions and engage in climate-friendly activities, check out these websites:

EPA- What you can do: http://www.epa.gov/climatechange/wycd/index.html

NPS- Climate Change Response Program: http://www.nps.gov/climatechange

NPS- Do Your Part! Program: http://www.nps.gov/climatefriendlyparks/doyourpart.html

US Forest Service Climate Change Program: http://www.fs.fed.us/climatechange/

United States Global Change Research Program: http://www.globalchange.gov/

U.S. Fish and Wildlife Service Climate change: http://www.fws.gov/home/climatechange/

The Climate Friendly Parks Program is a joint partnership between the U.S. Environmental Protection Agency and the National Park Service. Climate Friendly Parks from around the country are leading the way in the effort to protect our parks' natural and cultural resources and ensure their preservation for future generations; NPS image.

CLIMATE *Friendly* PARKS

IV. Global Climate Change

The IPCC is a scientific intergovernmental, international body established by the World Meteorological Organization (WMO) and by the United Nations Environment Programme (UNEP). The information the IPCC provides in its reports is based on scientific evidence and reflects existing consensus viewpoints within the scientific community. The comprehensiveness of the scientific content is achieved through contributions from experts in all regions of the world and all relevant disciplines including, where appropriately documented, industry literature and traditional practices, and a two stage review process by experts and governments.

Definition of climate change: The IPCC defines climate change as a change in the state of the climate that can be identified (e.g. using statistical tests) by changes in the mean and/or the variability of its properties, and that persists for an extended period, typically decades or longer. All statements in this section are synthesized from the IPCC report unless otherwise noted.

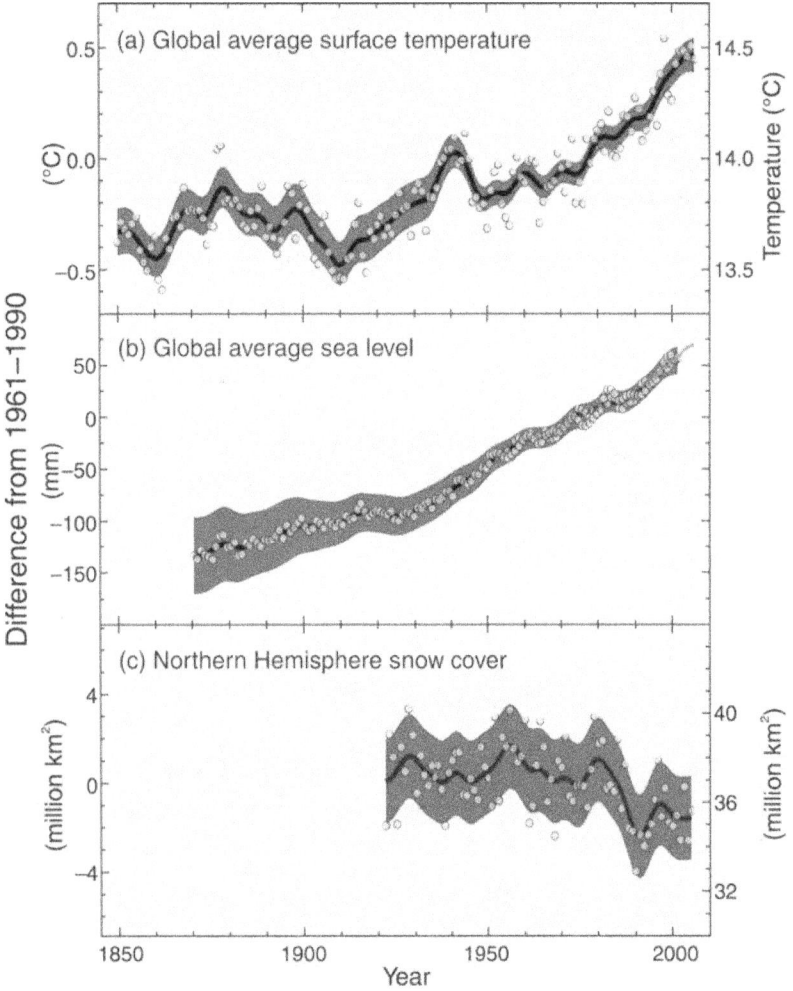

Figure 1. Observed changes in (a) global average surface temperature; (b) global average sea level from tide gauge (blue) and satellite (red) data and (c) Northern Hemisphere snow cover for March-April. All differences are relative to corresponding averages for the period 1961-1990. Smoothed curves represent decadal averaged values while circles show yearly values. The shaded areas are the uncertainty intervals estimated from a comprehensive analysis of known uncertainties (a and b) and from the time series (c) (IPCC 2007a).

A. Temperature and Greenhouse Gases

What scientists know...

- Warming of the Earth's climate system is unequivocal, as evidenced from increased air and ocean temperatures, widespread melting of snow and ice, and rising global average sea level (Figure 1).

- In the last 100 years, global average surface temperature has risen about 0.74°C over the previous 100-year period, and the rate of warming has doubled from the previous century. Eleven of the 12 warmest years in the instrumental record of global surface temperature since 1850 have occurred since 1995 (Figure 1).

- Although most regions over the globe have experienced warming, there are regional variations: land regions have warmed faster than oceans and high northern latitudes have warmed faster than the tropics. Average Arctic temperatures have increased at almost twice the global rate in the past 100 years, primarily because loss of snow and ice results in a positive feedback via increased absorption of sunlight by ocean waters (Figure 2).

- Over the past 50 years widespread changes in extreme temperatures have been observed, including a decrease in cold days and nights and an increase in the frequency of hot days, hot nights, and heat waves.

- Winter temperatures are increasing more rapidly than summer temperatures, particularly in the northern hemisphere, and

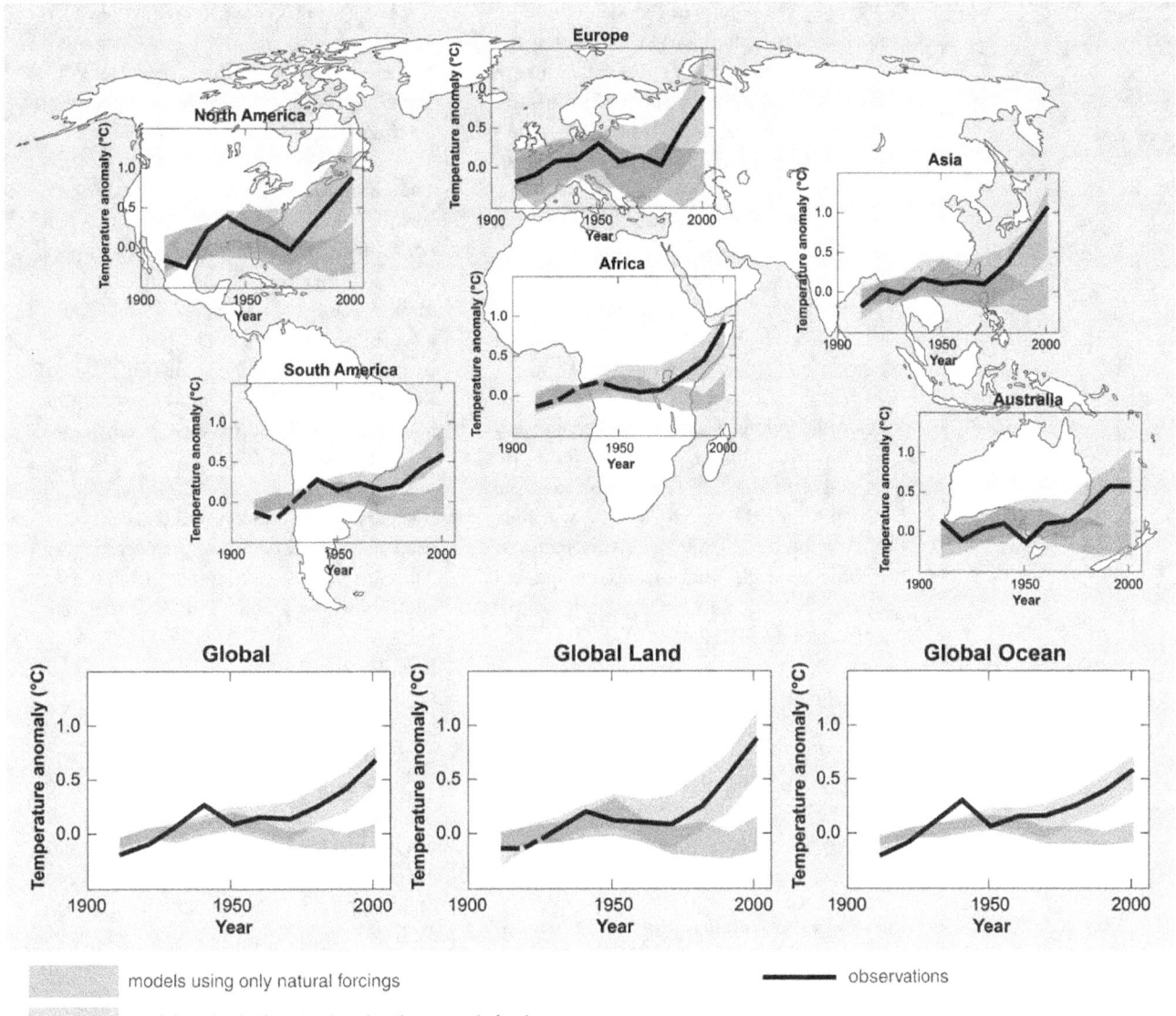

models using only natural forcings

models using both natural and anthropogenic forcings

—— observations

Figure 2. Comparison of observed continental- and global-scale changes in surface temperature with results simulated by climate models using either natural or both natural and anthropogenic forcings. Decadal averages of observations are shown for the period 1906-2005 (black line) plotted against the centre of the decade and relative to the corresponding average for the period 1901-1950. Lines are dashed where spatial coverage is less than 50%. Blue shaded bands show the 5 to 95% range for 19 simulations from five climate models using only the natural forcings due to solar activity and volcanoes. Red shaded bands show the 5 to 95% range for 58 simulations from 14 climate models using both natural and anthropogenic forcings (IPCC 2007a).

there has been an increase in the length of the frost-free period in mid- and high-latitude regions of both hemispheres.

- Climate change is caused by alterations in the energy balance within the atmosphere and at the Earth's surface. Factors that affect Earth's energy balance are the atmospheric concentrations of greenhouse gases and aerosols, land surface properties, and solar radiation.

- Global atmospheric concentrations of greenhouse gases have increased significantly since 1750 as the result of human activities. The principal greenhouse gases are carbon dioxide (CO_2), primarily from fossil fuel use and land-use change; methane (CH_4) and nitrous oxide (N_2O), primarily from agriculture; and halocarbons

(a group of gases containing fluorine, chlorine or bromine), principally engineered chemicals that do not occur naturally.

- Direct measurements of gases trapped in ice cores demonstrate that current CO_2 and CH_4 concentrations far exceed the natural range over the last 650,000 years and have increased markedly (35% and 148% respectively), since the beginning of the industrial era in 1750.

- Both past and future anthropogenic CO_2 emissions will continue to contribute to warming and sea level rise for more than a millennium, due to the time scales required for the removal of the gas from the atmosphere.

- Warming temperatures reduce oceanic up-take of atmospheric CO_2, increasing the fraction of anthropogenic emissions remaining in the atmosphere. This positive carbon cycle feedback results in increasingly greater accumulation of atmospheric CO_2 and subsequently greater warming trends than would otherwise be present in the absence of a feedback relationship.

- There is very high confidence that the global average net effect of human activities since 1750 has been one of warming.

- Scientific evidence shows that major and widespread climate changes have occurred with startling speed. For example, roughly half the north Atlantic warming during the last 20,000 years was achieved in only a decade, and it was accompanied by significant climatic changes across most of the globe (NRC 2008).

What scientists think is likely...

- Anthropogenic warming over the last three decades has likely had a discernible influence at the global scale on observed changes in many physical and biological systems.

- Average temperatures in the Northern Hemisphere during the second half of the 20th century were very likely higher than during any other 50-year period in the last 500 years and likely the highest in at least the past 1300 years.

- Most of the warming that has occurred since the mid-20th century is very likely due to increases in anthropogenic green-house gas concentrations. Furthermore, it is extremely likely that global changes observed in the past 50 years can only be explained with external (anthropogenic) forcings (influences) (Figure 2).

- There is much evidence and scientific consensus that greenhouse gas emissions will continue to grow under current climate change mitigation policies and development practices. For the next two decades a warming of about 0.2°C per decade is projected for a range of emissions scenarios; afterwards, temperature projections increasingly depend on specific emissions scenarios (Table 1).

- It is very likely that continued greenhouse gas emissions at or above the current rate will cause further warming and result in changes in the global climate system that will be larger than those observed during the 20th century.

- It is very likely that hot extremes, heat waves and heavy precipitation events will become more frequent. As with current trends, warming is expected to be greatest over land and at most high northern latitudes, and least over the Southern Ocean (near Antarctica) and the northern North Atlantic Ocean.

What scientists think is possible...

- Global temperatures are projected to increase in the future, and the magnitude of temperature change depends on specific emissions scenarios, and ranges from a 1.1°C to 6.4°C increase by 2100 (Table 1).

Table 1. Projected global average surface warming at the end of the 21st century, adapted from (IPCC 2007b).

Notes: a) Temperatures are assessed best estimates and likely uncertainty ranges from a hierarchy of models of varying complexity as well as observational constraints. b) Temperature changes are expressed as the difference from the period 1980-1999. To express the change relative to the period 1850-1899 add 0.5°C. c) Year 2000 constant composition is derived from Atmosphere-Ocean General Circulation Models (AOGCMs) only.

Emissions Scenario	Temperature Change (°C at 2090 – 2099 relative to 1980 – 1999)[a,b]	
	Best Estimate	Likely Range
Constant Year 2000 Concentrations[a]	0.6	0.3 – 0.9
B_1 Scenario	1.8	1.1 – 2.9
B_2 Scenario	2.4	1.4 – 3.8
A_1B Scenario	2.8	1.7 – 4.4
A_2 Scenario	3.4	2.0 – 5.4
A_1F_1 Scenario	4.0	2.4 – 6.4

Figure 3. Sea ice concentrations (the amount of ice in a given area) simulated by the GFDL CM2.1 global coupled climate model averaged over August, September and October (the months when Arctic sea ice concentrations generally are at a minimum). Three years (1885, 1985 & 2085) are shown to illustrate the model-simulated trend. A dramatic reduction of summertime sea ice is projected, with the rate of decrease being greatest during the 21st century portion. The colors range from dark blue (ice free) to white (100% sea ice covered); Image courtesy of NOAA GFDL.

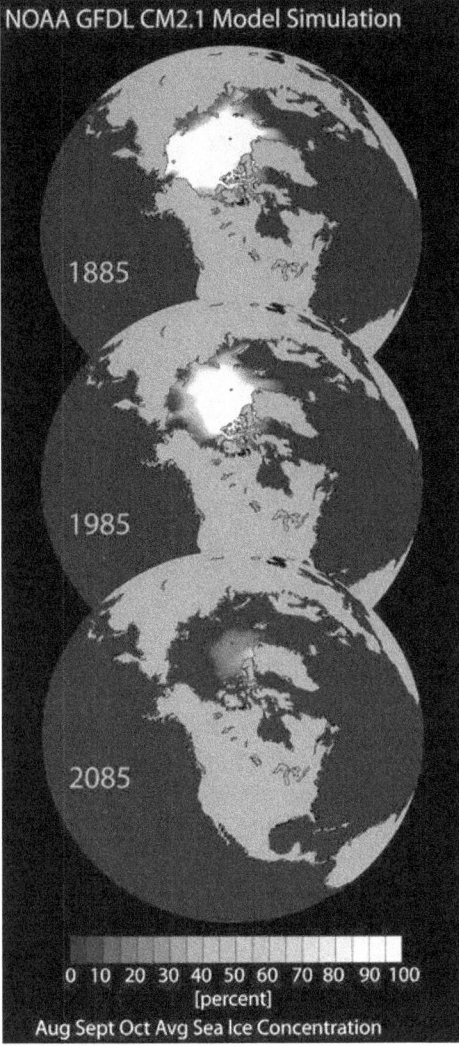

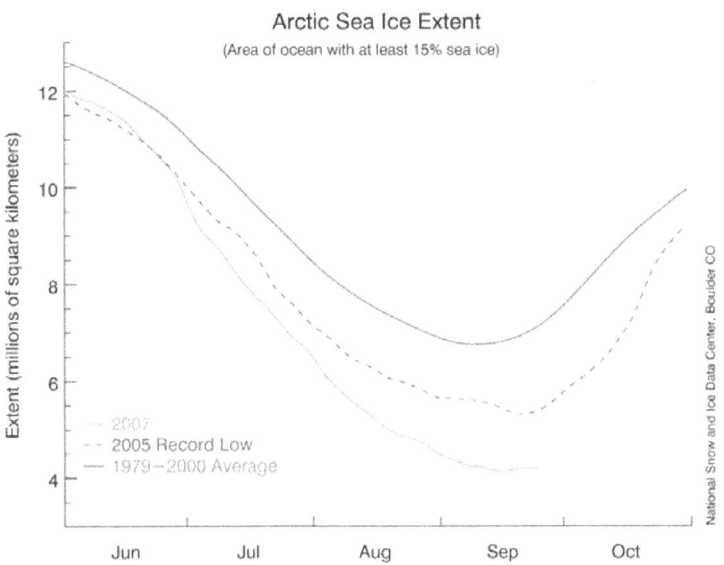

Figure 4. Arctic sea ice in September 2007 (blue line) is far below the previous low record year of 2005 (dashed line), and was 39% below where we would expect to be in an average year (solid gray line). Average September sea ice extent from 1979 to 2000 was 7.04 million square kilometers. The climatological minimum from 1979 to 2000 was 6.74 million square kilometers (NSIDC 2008).

- Anthropogenic warming could lead to changes in the global system that are abrupt and irreversible, depending on the rate and magnitude of climate change.

- Roughly 20-30% of species around the globe could become extinct if global average temperatures increase by 2 to 3°C over pre-industrial levels.

B. Water, Snow, and Ice

What scientists know...

- Many natural systems are already being affected by increased temperatures, particularly those related to snow, ice, and frozen ground. Examples are decreases in snow and ice extent, especially of mountain glaciers; enlargement and increased numbers of glacial lakes; decreased permafrost extent; increasing ground instability in permafrost regions and rock avalanches in mountain regions; and thinner sea ice and shorter freezing seasons of lake and river ice (Figure 3).

- Annual average Arctic sea ice extent has shrunk by 2.7% per decade since 1978, and the summer ice extent has decreased by 7.4% per decade. Sea ice extent during the 2007 melt season plummeted to the lowest levels since satellite measurements began in 1979, and at the end of the melt season September 2007 sea ice was 39% below the long-term (1979-2000) average (NSIDC 2008)(Figure 4).

- Global average sea level rose at an average rate of 1.8 mm per year from 1961 to 2003 and at an average rate of 3.1 mm per year from 1993 to 2003. Increases in sea level since 1993 are the result of the following contributions: thermal expansion, 57%; melting glaciers and ice caps, 28%, melting polar ice sheets, 15%.

- The CO_2 content of the oceans increased by 118 ± 19 Gt (1 Gt = 109 tons) between A.D. 1750 (the end of the pre-industrial period) and 1994 as the result of uptake of anthropogenic CO_2 emissions from the atmosphere, and continues to increase by about 2 Gt each year (Sabine et al. 2004; Hoegh-Guldberg et al. 2007). This increase in oceanic CO_2 has resulted in a 30% increase in acidity (a decrease in surface ocean pH by an average of 0.1 units), with observed and potential severe negative consequences for marine organisms and coral reef formations (Orr et al. 2005: McNeil and Matear 2007; Riebesell et al. 2009).

- Oceans are noisier due to ocean acidification reducing the ability of seawater to absorb low frequency sounds (noise from ship traffic and military activities). Low-frequency sound absorption has decreased over 10% in both the Pacific and Atlantic over the past 200 years. An assumed additional pH drop of 0.3 (due to anthropogenic CO_2 emissions) accompanied with warming will lead to sound absorption below 1 kHz being reduced by almost half of current values (Hester et. al. 2008).

- Even if greenhouse gas concentrations are stabilized at current levels thermal expansion of ocean waters (and resulting sea level rise) will continue for many centuries, due to the time required to transport heat into the deep ocean.

- Observations since 1961 show that the average global ocean temperature has increased to depths of at least 3000 meters, and that the ocean has been taking up over 80% of the heat added to the climate system.

- Hydrologic effects of climate change include increased runoff and earlier spring peak discharge in many glacier- and snow-fed rivers, and warming of lakes and rivers.

- Runoff is projected to increase by 10 to 40% by mid-century at higher latitudes and in some wet tropical areas, and to decrease by 10 to 30% over some dry regions at mid-latitudes and dry tropics. Areas in which runoff is projected to decline face a reduction in the value of the services provided by water resources.

- Precipitation increased significantly from 1900 to 2005 in eastern parts of North and South America, northern Europe, and northern and central Asia. Conversely, precipitation declined in the Sahel, the Mediterranean, southern Africa, and parts of southern Asia (Figure 5).

What scientists think is likely....

- Widespread mass losses from glaciers and reductions in snow cover are projected to accelerate throughout the 21st century, reducing water availability and changing seasonality of flow patterns.

- Model projections include contraction of snow cover area, widespread increases in depth to frost in permafrost areas, and Arctic and Antarctic sea ice shrinkage.

- The incidence of extreme high sea level has likely increased at a broad range of sites worldwide since 1975.

- Based on current model simulations it is very likely that the meridional overturning circulation (MOC) of the Atlantic Ocean will slow down during the 21st century; nevertheless regional temperatures are predicted to increase. Large-scale and persistent changes in the MOC may result in changes in marine ecosystem produc-

Figure 5. Relative changes in precipitation (in percent) for the period 2090-2099, relative to 1980-1999. Values are multi-model averages based on the SRES A$_1$B scenario for December to February (left) and June to August (right). White areas are where less than 66% of the models agree in the sign of the change and stippled areas are where more than 90% of the models agree in the sign of the change (IPCC 2007a).

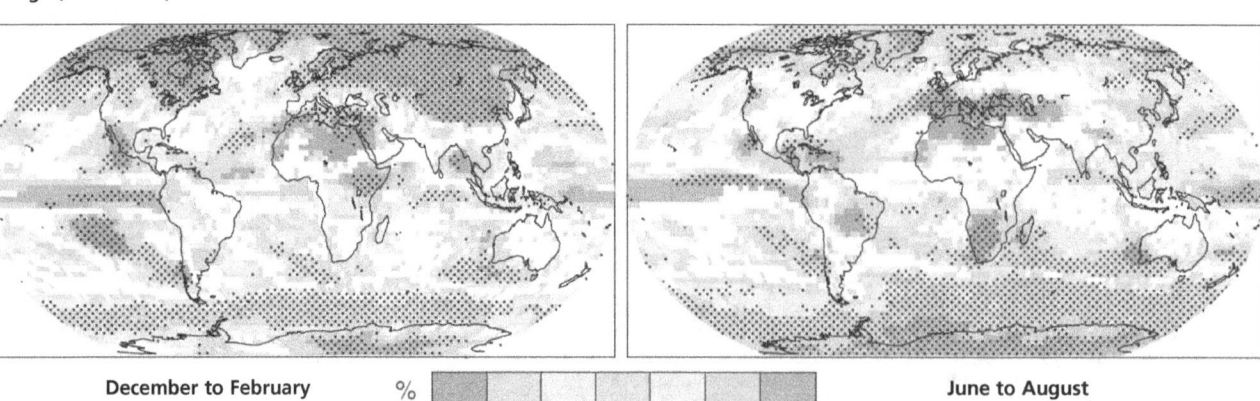

December to February   %   June to August

-20   -10   -5   5   10   20

Table 2. Projected global average sea level rise at the end of the 21st century, adapted from IPCC 2007b.

Notes: a) Temperatures are assessed best estimates and likely uncertainty ranges from a hierarchy of models of varying complexity as well as observational constraints.

Emissions Scenario	Sea level rise (m at 2090 – 2099 relative to 1980 – 1999)
	Model-based range (excluding future rapid dynamical changes in ice flow)
Constant Year 2000 Concentrations[a]	0.3 – 0.9
B₁ Scenario	1.1 – 2.9
B₂ Scenario	1.4 – 3.8
A₁B Scenario	1.7 – 4.4
A₂ Scenario	2.0 – 5.4
A₁F₁ Scenario	2.4 – 6.4

tivity, fisheries, ocean CO_2 uptake, and terrestrial vegetation.

- Globally the area affected by drought has likely increased since the 1970s and the frequency of extreme precipitation events has increased over most areas.

- Future tropical cyclones (typhoons and hurricanes) are likely to become more intense, with larger peak wind speeds and increased heavy precipitation. Extra-tropical storm tracks are projected to move poleward, with consequent shifts in wind, precipitation, and temperature patterns.

- Increases in the amount of precipitation are very likely in high latitudes and decreases are likely in most subtropical land regions, continuing observed patterns (Figure 5).

- Increases in the frequency of heavy precipitation events in the coming century are very likely, resulting in potential damage to crops and property, soil erosion, surface and groundwater contamination, and increased risk of human death and injury.

What scientists think is possible...

- Arctic late-summer sea ice may disappear almost entirely by the end of the 21st century (Figure 3).

- Current global model studies project that the Antarctic ice sheet will remain too cold for widespread surface melting and gain mass due to increased snowfall. However, net loss of ice mass could occur if dynami-

cal ice discharge dominates the ice sheet mass balance.

- Model-based projections of global average sea level rise at the end of the 21st century range from 0.18 to 0.59 meters, depending on specific emissions scenarios (Table 2). These projections may actually underestimate future sea level rise because they do not include potential feedbacks or full effects of changes in ice sheet flow.

- Partial loss of ice sheets and/or the thermal expansion of seawater over very long time scales could result in meters of sea level rise, major changes in coastlines and inundation of low-lying areas, with greatest effects in river deltas and low-lying islands.

C. Vegetation and Wildlife

What scientists know...

- Temperature increases have affected Arctic and Antarctic ecosystems and predator species at high levels of the food web.

- Changes in water temperature, salinity, oxygen levels, circulation, and ice cover in marine and freshwater ecosystems have resulted in shifts in ranges and changes in algal, plankton, and fish abundance in high-latitude oceans; increases in algal and zooplankton abundance in high-latitude and high-altitude lakes; and range shifts and earlier fish migrations in rivers.

- High-latitude (cooler) ocean waters are currently acidified enough to start dissolving pteropods; open water marine snails which are one of the primary food sources of young salmon and mackerel (Fabry et al. 2008, Feely et al. 2008). In lower latitude (warmer) waters, by the end of this century Humboldt squid's metabolic rate will be reduced by 31% and activity levels by 45% due to reduced pH, leading to squid retreating at night to shallower waters to feed and replenish oxygen levels (Rosa and Seibel 2008).

- A meta-analysis of climate change effects on range boundaries in Northern Hemisphere species of birds, butterflies, and alpine herbs shows an average shift of 6.1 kilometers per decade northward (or 6.1 meters per decade upward), and a mean shift toward earlier onset of spring events (frog breeding, bird nesting, first flowering, tree budburst, and arrival of migrant butterflies and birds) of 2.3 days per decade (Parmesan and Yohe 2003).

- Poleward range shifts of individual species and expansions of warm-adapted communities have been documented on all continents and in most of the major oceans of the world (Parmesan 2006).

- Satellite observations since 1980 indicate a trend in many regions toward earlier greening of vegetation in the spring linked to longer thermal growing seasons resulting from recent warming.

- Over the past 50 years humans have changed ecosystems more rapidly and extensively than in any previous period of human history, primarily as the result of growing demands for food, fresh water, timber, fiber, and fuel. This has resulted in a substantial and largely irreversible loss of Earth's biodiversity

- Although the relationships have not been quantified, it is known that loss of intact ecosystems results in a reduction in ecosystem services (clean water, carbon sequestration, waste decomposition, crop pollination, etc.).

What scientists think is likely...

- The resilience of many ecosystems is likely to be exceeded this century by an unprecedented combination of climate change, associated disturbance (flooding, drought, wildfire, insects, ocean acidification) and other global change drivers (land use change, pollution, habitat fragmentation, invasive species, resource over-exploitation) (Figure 6).

- Exceedance of ecosystem resilience may be characterized by threshold-type responses such as extinctions, disruption of ecological interactions, and major changes in ecosystem structure and disturbance regimes.

- Net carbon uptake by terrestrial ecosystems is likely to peak before mid-century and then weaken or reverse, amplifying climate changes. By 2100 the terrestrial biosphere is likely to become a carbon source.

- Increases in global average temperature above 1.5 to 2.5°C and concurrent atmospheric CO_2 concentrations are projected to result in major changes in ecosystem structure and function, species' ecological interactions, and species' geographical ranges. Negative consequences are projected for species biodiversity and ecosystem goods and services.

- Model projections for increased atmospheric CO_2 concentration and global temperatures significantly exceed values for at least the past 420,000 years, the period during which more extant marine organisms evolved. Under expected 21st century conditions it is likely that global warming and ocean acidification will compromise carbonate accretion, resulting in less diverse reef communities and failure of some existing carbonate reef structures. Climate changes will likely exacerbate local stresses from declining water quality and overexploitation of key species (Hoegh-Guldberg et al. 2007).

- Ecosystems likely to be significantly impacted by changing climatic conditions include:

i. Terrestrial – tundra, boreal forest, and mountain regions (sensitivity to warming); Mediterranean-type ecosystems and tropical rainforests (decreased rainfall)

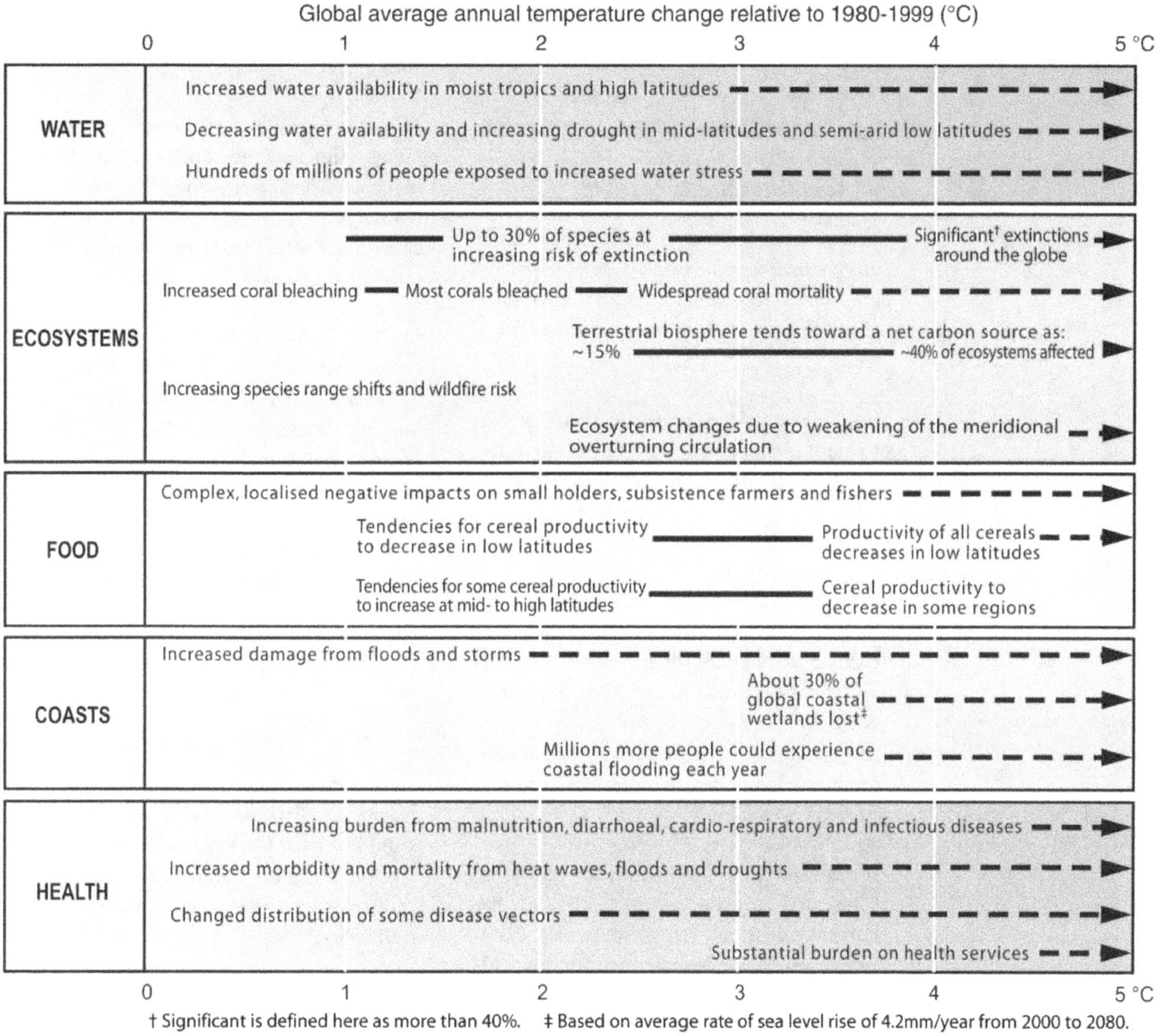

Global average annual temperature change relative to 1980-1999 (°C)

0 1 2 3 4 5 °C

WATER
- Increased water availability in moist tropics and high latitudes
- Decreasing water availability and increasing drought in mid-latitudes and semi-arid low latitudes
- Hundreds of millions of people exposed to increased water stress

ECOSYSTEMS
- Up to 30% of species at increasing risk of extinction — Significant[†] extinctions around the globe
- Increased coral bleaching — Most corals bleached — Widespread coral mortality
- Terrestrial biosphere tends toward a net carbon source as: ~15% — ~40% of ecosystems affected
- Increasing species range shifts and wildfire risk
- Ecosystem changes due to weakening of the meridional overturning circulation

FOOD
- Complex, localised negative impacts on small holders, subsistence farmers and fishers
- Tendencies for cereal productivity to decrease in low latitudes — Productivity of all cereals decreases in low latitudes
- Tendencies for some cereal productivity to increase at mid- to high latitudes — Cereal productivity to decrease in some regions

COASTS
- Increased damage from floods and storms
- About 30% of global coastal wetlands lost[‡]
- Millions more people could experience coastal flooding each year

HEALTH
- Increasing burden from malnutrition, diarrhoeal, cardio-respiratory and infectious diseases
- Increased morbidity and mortality from heat waves, floods and droughts
- Changed distribution of some disease vectors
- Substantial burden on health services

0 1 2 3 4 5 °C

† Significant is defined here as more than 40%.   ‡ Based on average rate of sea level rise of 4.2mm/year from 2000 to 2080.

Warming by 2090-2099 relative to 1980-1999 for non-mitigation scenarios

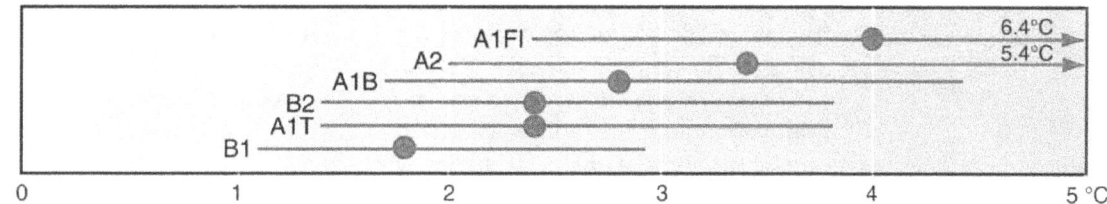

A1FI — 6.4°C
A2 — 5.4°C
A1B
B2
A1T
B1

0 1 2 3 4 5 °C

Figure 6. Examples of impacts associated with projected global average surface warming. Upper panel: Illustrative examples of global impacts projected for climate changes (and sea level and atmospheric CO_2 where relevant) associated with different amounts of increase in global average surface temperature in the 21st century. The black lines link impacts; broken-line arrows indicate impacts continuing with increasing temperature. Entries are placed so that the left-hand side of text indicates the approximate level of warming that is associated with the onset of a given impact. Quantitative entries for water scarcity and flooding represent the additional impacts of climate change relative to the conditions projected across the range of SRES scenarios A1FI, A2, B1 and B2. Adaptation to climate change is not included in these estimations. Confidence levels for all statements are high. Lower panel: Dots and bars indicate the best estimate and likely ranges of warming assessed for the six SRES marker scenarios for 2090-2099 relative to 1980-1999 (IPCC 2007a).

ii. Coastal – mangroves and salt marshes (multiple stresses)

iii. Marine – coral reefs (multiple stresses); sea-ice biomes (sensitivity to warming)

What scientists think is possible...

- Approximately 20% to 30% of plant and animal species assessed to date are at increased risk of extinction with increases in global average temperature in excess of 1.5 to 2.5°C.

- Endemic species may be more vulnerable to climate changes, and therefore at higher risk for extinction, because they may have evolved in locations where paleo-climatic conditions have been stable.

- Although there is great uncertainty about how forests will respond to changing climate and increasing levels of atmospheric CO_2, the factors that are most typically predicted to influence forests are increased fire, increased drought, and greater vulnerability to insects and disease (Brown 2008).

- If atmospheric CO_2 levels reach 450 ppm (projected to occur by 2030–2040 at the current emissions rates), reefs may experience rapid and terminal decline worldwide from multiple climate change-related direct and indirect effects including mass bleaching, ocean acidification, damage to shallow reef communities,reduction of biodiversity, and extinctions. (Veron et al. 2009). At atmospheric CO_2 levels of 560 ppmv, calcification of tropical corals is expected to decline by 30%, and loss of coral structure in areas of high erosion may outpace coral growth. With unabated CO_2 emissions, 70% of the presently known reef locations (including cold-water corals) will be in corrosive waters by the end of this century (Riebesell, et al. 2009).

D. Disturbance

What scientists know...

- Climate change currently contributes to the global burden of disease and premature death through exposure to extreme events and changes in water and air quality, food quality and quantity, ecosystems, agriculture, and economy (Parry et al. 2007).

- The most vulnerable industries, settlements, and societies are generally those in coastal and river flood plains, those whose economies are closely linked with climate-sensitive resources, and those in areas prone to extreme weather events.

- By 2080-2090 millions more people than today are projected to experience flooding due to sea level rise, especially those in the low-lying megadeltas of Asia and Africa and on small islands.

- Climate change affects the function and operation of existing water infrastructure and water management practices, aggravating the impacts of population growth, changing economic activity, land-use change, and urbanization.

What scientists think is likely...

- Up to 20% of the world's population will live in areas where river flood potential could increase by 2080-2090, with major consequences for human health, physical infrastructure, water quality, and resource availability.

- The health status of millions of people is projected to be affected by climate change, through increases in malnutrition; increased deaths, disease, and injury due to extreme weather events; increased burden of diarrheal diseases; increased cardio-respiratory disease due to higher concentrations of ground-level ozone in urban areas; and altered spatial distribution of vector-borne diseases.

- Risk of hunger is projected to increase at lower latitudes, especially in seasonally dry and tropical regions.

What scientists think is possible...

- Although many diseases are projected to increase in scope and incidence as the result of climate changes, lack of appropriate longitudinal data on climate change-related health impacts precludes definitive assessment.

V. References

Anderson, W.L., D.M. Robertson, and J.J. Magnuson. (1996). Evidence of recent warming and El Niño-related variations in ice breakup of Wisconsin lakes. Limnology and Oceanography, 41: 815-821. Available at http://aslo.org/lo/toc/vol_41/issue_5/0815.pdf (accessed 25 June 2007).

Austin, J. A., and S. M. Colman. (2007). Lake Superior summer water temperatures are increasing more rapidly than regional air temperatures: A positive ice-albedo feedback, Geophysical Research Letters, 34(6).

Bridgeman, T. B., D. W. Schloesser, and A. E. Krause. (2006). Recruitment of hexagenia Mayfly Nymphs in Western Lake Erie Linked to Environmental Variability, Ecological Applications, 16(2), 601-611.

Brown, R. (2008). The implications of climate change for conservation, restoration, and management of National Forest lands. National Forest Restoration Collaborative.

Burns, C. E., K.M. Johnston, and O.J. Schmitz. (2003). Global climate change and mammalian species diversity in U.S. National Parks. Proceedings of the National Academy of Sciences of the United States of America. 100(20): 11474-11477. Available at: http://www.pnas.org/cgi/reprint/100/20/11474.pdf (accessed 25 June 2007).

Desai, A. R., J. A. Austin, V. Bennington, and G. A. McKinley. (2009). Stronger winds over a large lake in response to weakening air-to-lake temperature gradient, Nature Geoscience, 2, 855-858.

Dobiesz, N. E., and N. P. Lester. (2009). Changes in Mid-Summer Water Temperature and Clarity Across the Great Lakes between 1968 and 2002, Journal of Great Lakes Research, 35(3), 371-384.

Fabry, V.J, B.A. Seibel, R.A. Feely, and J.C. Orr. (2008). Impacts of ocean acidification on marine fauna and ecosystem processes. ICES Journal of Marine Science 65: 414-432.

Feely, R.A., C.L. Sabine, J. M. Hernandez-Ayon, D. Lanson and B. Hales. (2008). Evidence for upwelling of corrosive "acidified" water onto the continental shelf. Science 320(5882): 1490-1492.

Finucane, M. L. (2009). Why Science Alone Won't Solve the Climate Crisis: Managing Climate Risks in the PacificRep., 8 pp.

Fitzpatrick, M., and W. Hargrove. (2009). The projection of species distribution models and the problem of non-analog climate, Biodiversity and Conservation, 18(8), 2255-2261.

Frelich, L. E., and P. B. Reich. (2009). Wilderness Conservation in an Era of Global Warming and Invasive Species: A Case Study from Minnesota's Boundary Waters Canoe Area Wilderness, Natural Areas Journal, 29(4), 385-393.

Hanrahan, J. L., S. V. Kravtsov, and P. J. Roebber. (2010). Connecting past and present climate variability to the water levels of Lakes Michigan and Huron, Geophys. Res. Lett., 37(1), L01701.

Hayhoe, K., C. Wake, T. Huntington, L. Luo, M. Schwartz, J. Sheffield, E. Wood, B. Anderson, J. Bradbury, A. DeGaetano, T. Troy, and D. Wolfe. (2007). Past and future changes in climate and hydrological indicators in the US Northeast. Climate Dynamics 28: 381-407. Abstract available at: http://www.ingentaconnect.com/content/klu/382/2007/0000002 8/00000004/00000187?crawler=true (accessed 25 June 2007).

Henne, P. D., F. S. Hu, and D. T. Cleland. (2007). Lake-effect snow as the dominant control of mesic-forest distribution in Michigan, USA, Journal of Ecology, 95(3), 517-529.

Hester, K. C., E. T. Peltzer, W. J. Kirkwood and P. G. Brewer. (2008). "Unanticipated consequences of ocean acidification: A noisier ocean at lower pH." Geophysical Research Letters 35: L19601.

Hoegh-Guldberg, O., P. J. Mumby, A. J. Hooten, R. S. Steneck, P. Greenfield, E. Gomez, C. D. Harvell, P. F. Sale, A. J. Edwards, and K. Caldeira. (2007). Coral reefs under rapid climate change and ocean acidification. Science 318:1737.

Howk, F. (2009). Changes in Lake Superior ice cover at Bayfield, Wisconsin, Journal of Great Lakes Research, 35(1), 159-162.

IPCC (2008). Climate Change and WaterRep., 210 pp, IPCC Secretariat, Geneva.

IPCC (Intergovernmental Panel on Climate Change). (2007a). Climate Change 2007: The Physical Science Basis. Contribution of Working Group I to the Fourth Assessment Report of the Intergovernmental Panel on Climate Change [IPCC, S., D. Qin, M. Manning, Z. Chen, M. Marquis, K.B. Averyt, M. Tignor and H.L. Miller, editors.] Cambridge University Press, Cambridge, United Kingdom and New York, NY, USA, 996 pp. Available at http://ipcc-wg1.ucar.edu/wg1/wg1-report.html (accessed 26 June 2007).

IPCC (Intergovernmental Panel on Climate Change). (2007b). Climate Change 2007 - Impacts, Adaptation and Vulnerability: Working Group II contribution to the Fourth Assessment Report of the Intergovernmental Panel on Climate Change (Climate Change 2007) [Adger, N. et al., editors]. Cambridge University Press, New York. Available at: http://www.ipcc.ch/SPM13apr07.pdf (accessed 3 July 2007).

Iverson, L. R. and A. M. Prasad. (2002). Potential redistribution of trees species habitat under five climate change scenarios in the eastern US. Forest Ecology and Management 155: 205-222. Available at: http://www.fs.fed.us/ne/newtown_square/publications/other_publishers/OCR/ne_2002_iverson001.pdf (accessed 26 June 2007).

Iverson, L. R., M. W. Schwartz and A. M. Prasad. (2004). Potential colonization of newly available tree-species habitat under climate change: an analysis for five eastern US species. Landscape Ecology 19: 787-799. Available at: http://www.fs.fed.us/ne/newtown_square/publications/other_publishers/OCR/ne_2004_iverson002.pdf (accessed 26 June 2007).

Kling , G.W., K. Hayhoe, L.B. Johnson, J.J. Magnuson, S. Polasky, S.K. Robinson, B.J. Shuter, M.M. Wander, D.J. Wuebbles, D.R. Zak, R.L. Lindroth, S.C. Moser, and M.L. Wilson. (2003). Confronting climate change in the Great Lakes Region. Union of Concerned Scientists, Cambridge, Massachusetts, and Ecological Society of America, Washington, D.C. Available at http://www.ucsusa.org/assets/documents/global_warming/greatlakes_final.pdf (accessed 26 June 2007).

Lehman, J.T. (2002). Mixing patterns and plankton biomass of the St. Lawrence Great Lakes under climate change scenarios. Journal of Great Lakes Research 28(4): 583-596. Available at http://www.iaglr.org/jglr/db/view_contents.php?pub_id=1995&mode=view&table=yes&topic_id=48&mode=topic_section&volume=28&issue=4 (accessed 26 June 2007).

Lofgren, B. M., F.H. Quinn, A.H. Clites, R.A. Assel, A.J. Eberhardt, and C.L. Luukkonen. (2002). Evaluation of potential impacts on Great Lakes water resources based on climate scenarios of two global circulation models. Journal of Great Lakes Research 28(4): 537-554. Abstract available at http://www.glerl.noaa.gov/pubs/fulltext/2002/20020020.pdf (accessed 26 June 2007).

Magnuson, J.J., D.M. Robertson, B.J. Benson, R.H. Wynne, D.M. Livingstone, T. Arai, R.A. Assel, R.G. Barry, V. Card, E. Kuusisto, N.G. Granin, T.D. Prowse, K.M. Stewart, and V.S. Vuglinski. (2000). Historical trends in lake and river ice cover in the Northern Hemisphere. Science 289: 1743-1746. Abstract available at http://www.sciencemag.org/cgi/content/abstract/289/5485/1743 (accessed 26 June 2007).

Malkin, S. Y., S. J. Guilford, and R. E. Hecky. (2008). Modeling the growth response of Cladophora in a Laurentian Great Lake to the exotic invader Dreissena and to lake warming, LIMNOL. OCEANOGR., 53(3), 1111-1124.

McBean, E., and H. Motiee. (2008). Assessment of impact of climate change on water resources: a long term analysis of the Great Lakes of North America, Hydrol. Earth Syst. Sci., 12(1), 239-255.

McNeil, B. I. and R. J. Matear. (2007). Climate change feedbacks on future oceanic acidification. Tellus 59B: 191–198.

NABCI (2010). The State of the Birds 2010 Report on Climate Change United States. The State of the Birds. A. F. King. Washington, DC, Department of the Interior, North American Bird Conservation Initiative.

NRC. (2008). Ecological impacts of climate change. The National Academies Press, Washington, D.C.

NRC. (2002). Abrupt climate change, inevitable surprises. National Academy Press, Washington, DC. 244 pp. Available at http://newton.nap.edu/catalog/10136.html#toc (accessed 26 June 2007).NSIDC. 2008. National Snow and Ice Data Center.

National Assessment Synthesis Team (NAST). (2000). Climate change impacts on the United States: the potential consequences of climate variability and change. US Global Change Research Program. Washington DC. Available at http://www.usgcrp.gov/usgcrp/Library/nationalassessment/overview.htm (accessed 26 June 2007).

Nicholls, R.J., and F.J.T. Klein. (2005). Climate change and coastal management of Europe's coast in F. Allan, U. Forstner, W. Salomons, J. Vermaat, M. Salomons, L. Bouwer, and K. Turner. Managing European coasts – past, present, and future. SpringerLink Berlin. Pages 199-226. Abstract available at: www.springerlink.com/content/j7x86g24370780k0/ (accessed 14 August 2007).

Novotny, E. V., and H. G. Stefan. (2007). Stream flow in Minnesota: Indicator of climate change, Journal of Hydrology, 334(3-4), 319-333.

Parmesan, C. (2006). Ecological and evolutionary responses to recent climate change. Annual Review of Ecology, Evolution, and Systematics 37: 637-669. Available at: http://cns.utexas.edu/communications/File/AnnRev_CCimpacts2006.pdf (accessed 26 June 2007).

Parmesan, C. and G. Yohe. (2003). A globally coherent fingerprint of climate change impacts across natural systems. Nature 421:37-42. Abstract available at http://www.nature.com/nature/journal/v421/n6918/abs/nature01286.html (accessed 26 June 2007).

Parry, M. L., O. F. Canziani, J. P. Palutikof, and Co-authors. (2007). Technical Summary. Climate Change 2007: Impacts, Adaptation and Vulnerability. Contribution of Working Group II to the Fourth Assessment Report of the Intergovernmental Panel on Climate Change, M.L. Parry, O.F. Canziani, J.P. Palutikof, P.J. van der Linden and C.E. Hanson, Eds., Cambridge University Press, Cambridge, UK, 23-78.

Patz, J. A., S. J. Vavrus, C. K. Uejio, and S. L. McLellan. (2008). Climate Change and Waterborne Disease Risk in the Great Lakes Region of the U.S, American journal of preventive medicine, 35(5), 451-458.

Patz, J., M. McGeehin, S. Bernard, K. Ebi, P. Epstein, A. Grambsch, D. Gubler, P. Reither, I. Romieu, J. Rose, J. Samet, and J. Trtanj. (2000). The potential health impacts of climate vulnerability and change for the United States: executive summary of the report of the U.S. national assessment. Environmental Health Perspectives 108/4: 367-376. Available at: http://www.pubmedcentral.nih.gov/articlerender.fcgi?artid=1638004 (accessed 16 July 2007).

Pendleton, E. A., E. R. Thieler, and S. J. Williams. (2010). Importance of Coastal Change Variables in Determining Vulnerability to Sea- and Lake-Level Change, Journal of Coastal Research, 26(1), 176-183.

Poff, N. L., M.M. Brimson, and J.W. Day, Jr. (2002). Aquatic ecosystems and global climate change: potential impacts on inland freshwater and coastal wetland ecosystems in the United States. Pew Center on Global Climate Change. Available at: http://www.pewclimate.org/docUploads/aquatic%2Epdf (accessed 26 June 2007).

Prasad, A. M. and L. R. Iverson. (2007). A climate change atlas for 80 forest tree species of the eastern United States [database]. Northeastern Research. http://www.nrs.fs.fed.us/atlas/ (accessed 26 June 2007).

Pruski, F.F., and M.A. Nearing. (2002). Climate-induced changes in erosion during the 21st century for eight U.S. locations. Water Resources Research 38/12: 1298. Available at: www.agu.org/pubs/crossref/2002/2001WR000493.shtml (accessed 13 August 2007).

Reither, P. (2001). Climate change and mosquito-borne disease. Environmental Health Perspectives 109: 141-161. Abstract available at: http://www.ncbi.nlm.nih.gov/sites/entrez?cmd=Retrieve&db=PubMed&list_uids=11250812&dopt=Abstract (accessed 26 June 2007).

Riebesell, U., A. Kortzinger and A. Oschlies. (2009). Sensitivities of marine carbon fluxes to ocean change. Proceedings of the National Academy of Sciences 106(49): 20602–20609.

Robertson, D. M., R.A. Ragotzkie, and J.J. Magnuson. (1992). Lake ice records used to detect historical and future climatic changes. Climatic Change 21:407-427. Abstract available at: http://www.springerlink.com/content/m7950303747854w7/ (accessed 26 June 2007).

Rosa, R. and B.A. Seibel. (2008). Synergistic effects of climate-related variables suggest future physiological impairment in a top oceanic predator. PNAS 105(52): 20776-20780.

Roy, E. D., J. F. Martin, E. G. Irwin, J. D. Conroy, and D. A. Culver. (2010). Transient social–ecological stability: the effects of invasive species and ecosystem restoration on nutrient management compromise in Lake Erie, Ecology and Society 15(1), 20.

Sabine, C. L., R. A. Feely, N. Gruber, R. M. Key, K. Lee, J. L. Bullister, R. Wanninkhof, C. S. Wong, D. W. R. Wallace, B. Tilbrook, F. J. Millero, T.-H. Peng, A. Kozyr, T. Ono and A. F. Rios. (2004). The Oceanic Sink for Anthropogenic CO2. 2004 305: 367-371.

Scott, D., J. Dawson, and B. Jones. (2008). Climate change vulnerability of the US Northeast winter recreation– tourism sector, Mitigation and Adaptation Strategies for Global Change, 13(5), 577-596.

Sharma, S., D. A. Jackson, C. K. Minns, and B. J. Shuter. (2007). Will northern fish populations be in hot water because of climate change?, Global Change Biology, 13(10), 2052-2064.

Smith, J. B., R. Richels, and B. Miller. (2001). Chapter 8: Potential consequences of climate variability and change for the Western United States, in Climate Change Impacts on the United States: The Potential Consequences of Climate Variability and Change. National Assessment Foundation Report, National Assessment Synthesis Team, edited, pp. 219-245, US Global Change Research Program.

Thompson, J. D., M.D. Flannigan, B.M. Wotton, R. Suffling. (1998). The effects of climate change on landscape diversity: an example in Ontario forests. Environmental Monitoring and Assessment 49: 213-233. Abstract available at: http://www.ingentaconnect.com/content/klu/emas/1998/00000049/F0020002/00145032 (accessed 26 June 2007).

Tobin, P. C., S. Nagarkatti, G. Loeb, and M. C. Saunders. (2008). Historical and projected interactions between climate change and insect voltinism in a multivoltine species, Global Change Biology, 14(5), 951-957.

Trumpickas, J., B. J. Shuter, and C. K. Minns. (2009). Forecasting impacts of climate change on Great Lakes surface water temperatures, Journal of Great Lakes Research, 35(3), 454-463.

Tucker, G.E., and R. Slingerland. (1997). Drainage basin responses to climate change. Water Resources Research 33/8:2031-2047. Available at: www.colorado.edu/geolsci/gtucker/preprints/tuckslingwrr97.pdf (accessed 14 August 2007).

UCS (Union of Concerned Scientists). (2006). Global warming 101: 2005 vies for hottest year on record. Available at http://www.ucsusa.org/global_warming/science/recordtemp2005.html (accessed 26 June 2007).

UNESCO (2007), Climate Change and World HeritageRep., 51 pp, UNESCO World Heritage Centre, Vilnius, Lithuania.

USDA (United States Department of Agriculture). (2001). Forests: the potential consequences of climate variability and change. A report of the National Forest assessment group for the U.S. Global Change Research Program. Available at http://www.usgcrp.gov/usgcrp/Library/nationalassessment/forests/forest.pdf (accessed 26 June 2007).

USGCRP (2009), Global Climate Change Impacts in the United StatesRep., United States Global Change Research Program.

USGCRP (US Global Change Science Research Program). (1996). The ecological effects of global warming on North American birds and butterflies. Overview: Terry Root. Seminar, 22 October 1996. Available at: http://www.usgcrp.gov/usgcrp/seminars/961010DD.html (accessed 26 June 2007).

Veron, J. E. N., O. Hoegh-Guldberg, T. M. Lenton, J. M. Lough, D. O. Obura, P. Pearce-Kelly, C. R. C. Sheppard, M. Spalding, M. G. Stafford-Smith and A. D. Rogers. (2009). The coral reef crisis: The critical importance of <350 ppm CO2. Marine Pollution Bulletin 58: 1428–1436.

Wall, G. (2008), The Tourism Industry and its Adaptability and Vulnerability to Climate Change.

Watson, R.T., M.C.Zinyowera, and R.H.Moss, editors. (1996). Impacts, adaptations and mitigations of climate change: Scientific-technical analyses. Intergovernmental Panel on Climate Change. New York: Cambridge University Press, Cambridge, UK.

Watson, R.T., M.C.Zinyowera, and R.H.Moss, editors. (1997). Intergovernmental Panel on Climate Change (IPCC). 1998. The regional impacts of climate change: an assessment of vulnerability. Intergovernmental Panel on Climate Change. New York: Cambridge University Press, Cambridge, UK. Cambridge University Press, Cambridge, UK.

Westerling, A. L., H. G. Hidalgo, D. R. Cayan, and T. W. Swetnam. (2006). Warming and earlier spring increases western U.S. forest wildfire activity. SciencExpress 2006(July 6):1-9. Available at: http://www.sciencemag.org/cgi/content/full/313/5789/940 (accessed 27 June 2007).

Winnet, S. M. (1998). Potential effects of climate change on U.S. forests: a review. Climate Research 11: 39-49. Available at: http://www.int-res.com/articles/cr/11/c011p039.pdf (accessed 26 June 2007).

Winter, T.C. (2000). The vulnerability of wetlands to climate change: a hydrologic landscape perspective. Journal of the American Water Resources Association 35/2: 305-311. Available at: www.blackwell-synergy.com/doi/abs/10.1111/j.1752-1688.2000.tb04269.x?journalCode=jawr (accessed 14 August 14, 2007).

Wuebbles, D. L. and K. Hayhoe. (2003). Climate Change Projections for the United States Midwest. Mitigation and Adaptation Strategies for Global Change 9: 335-363. Abstract available at: http://www.springerlink.com/content/k066717671581161/ (accessed 26 June 2007).

The Department of the Interior protects and manages the nation's natural resources and cultural heritage; provides scientific and other information about those resources; and honors its special responsibilities to American Indians, Alaska Natives, and affiliated Island Communities.

NPS 920/105620, September 2010